Charles University
Karolinum Press

PRAGUE

UNIVERSITY TOWN

Josef Petráň and Lydia Petráňová
Translated by Ian Finlay Stone

Karolinum Press

Originally published in Czech as *Praha univerzitní*, Prague: Karolinum, 2018
KAROLINUM PRESS, Ovocný trh 560/5, 116 36 Prague 1, Czech Republic
Karolinum Press is a publishing department of Charles University
www.karolinum.cz

ISBN 978-80-246-4053-2

The manuscript was reviewed by Professor Jan Royt (Institute of Art History, Faculty of Arts,
Charles University), Professor Jiří Pešek (Department of European Cultural and Intellectual History,
Faculty of Humanities, Charles University), expert consultant: Professor Petr Svobodný
(Institute of the History and Archive of Charles University)

The Prague series is edited by Milada Motlová

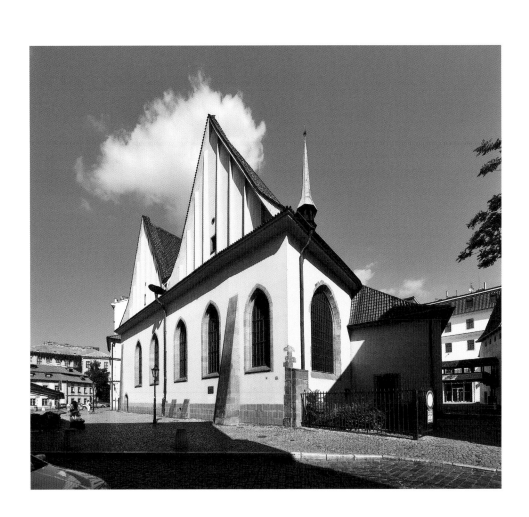

CONTENTS

PRAGUE:
UNIVERSITY TOWN

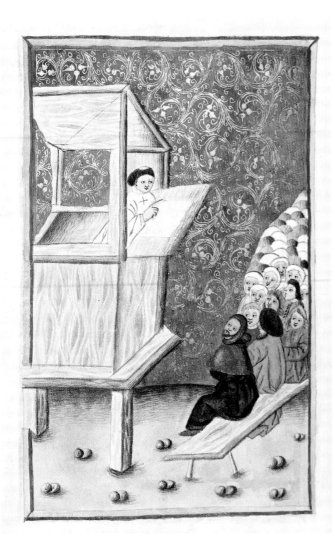

The exalted Latin passages of the founding charter of Charles University, which communicated the decision of Charles IV, king of Bohemia, king of the Holy Roman Empire and future emperor, to adorn the Kingdom of Bohemia with a 'large quantity of learned men' and to found in Prague the first university north of the Rhine, have already been recalled many times. Certainly the talented ruler, educated politician and diplomat was realistically following pragmatic aims when he allowed the foundation of a *studium generale* (general studies) in the kingdom's metropolis, which he intended to turn into a dignified centre of the Holy Roman Empire. In the founding charter, after praising the Czech Lands and their loyal inhabitants, whom he assures of his continued favour, King Charles IV also poured praise on the city of Prague itself. *Thus, to ensure that this beneficial and praiseworthy intention of our mind bear proper fruit and that the grandeur of this kingdom be augmented by numerous works of novelty, we have decided, after due consideration, to establish, elevate and newly create a studium generale in our metropolitan and particularly charming town of Prague, which, abounding in the riches of earthly crops, as well as the sweetness of the place and everything necessary, is exceedingly suitable and fit for such a grand task...*

In the first era up until the end of the 14th century, during which time Prague general studies (university, higher learning) remained without serious competition in central and eastern Europe, it attracted both teachers and students from a wide area of Europe. Within the framework of the academic community and the corporations of its faculties, four so-called university nations were created: Bohemian, Polish, Bavarian and Saxon. Each of these so-called nations, which were regional and not national corporations, had one vote in the election of academic representatives. They influenced appointments to the colleges of doctors and masters. This soon led to disputes, especially, as is always the case, when this concerned the sharing out of profits and careers bestowing power. In the end Wenceslas IV decided the matter with the Kutná Hora Decree, issued on 18 January 1409, which gave a threefold predominance to the Czech nation. The ruler's act, motivated by state interests, essentially interfered in the university's legal and administrative autonomy and immunity, and thus fundamentally signalled its entire future development.

The tradition of medieval higher learning in the sphere of West European Christendom was formed over many years, through the gradual improvement of statutory establishments. The task of the university was to educate in the widest sense of the word, to be morally formative and to spread knowledge at the highest attainable level. We should recall that the idea of a university did not comprise merely the acquiring of professional knowledge and skills, and the responsibility to use these practically in one's personal and social life. The primary duty of the university community was to search for truth. This truth was understood as God's truth, communicated and discovered by the interpretation of the bible and the teachings of the Holy Fathers. Neither was the moral and logical inheritance of the philosophers and learned men of antiquity neglected.

Bust of Emperor and King Charles IV, founder of higher learning in Prague, on the triforium of St. Vitus Cathedral. A work from Peter Parler's workshop in the years 1375–1380.

The culture of West European Christendom was founded on this spiritual inheritance. The intellectual elite – the university doctors and masters – were not supposed merely to transfer their acquired knowledge to the social environment outside of the university so that it could be used in everyday praxis; they were supposed to spread the sum of their acquired knowledge, directed toward a distant horizon which could not be fully seen, much further. In addition, they were supposed to transpose this sum of knowledge into higher cultural and moral values influencing society, to attempt to interpret and understand the world, to contribute to the welfare of its population, and to find their place in this world. This conception connects the medieval idea of the university with the modern age in spite of all the fundamental historical changes of systems and paradigms.

A learned person's acquisition of a universal spirit through university study was confirmed by the awarding of titles. The highest attainable scientific-pedagogical title in the Middle Ages was that of doctor – teacher, explicator. They were addressed as *honorabiles* (honoured). It was the duty of a doctor to pass on to pupils his own acquired knowledge in a mutual dialogue. The Faculty of Liberal Arts (Faculty of Arts), at which students usually began their university studies, was also the largest in terms of teacher and student numbers. The title attained here and confirmed by a diploma was that of *magister* – master of liberal arts. A substantial number of students left this faculty already after attaining the lower rank of *bacalaureus* (bachelor) to take up posts at lower-level municipal schools or various administrative functions for which an education was necessary.

An academic rank (degree), confirmed at the end of studies by a diploma, was recognized at all universities in the West European Christian sphere, and thus students were able to move freely from one university to another: this was the case of students who followed their teachers or who sought out renowned explicators, on condition of course that they properly paid their registration and tuition fees, as well

Foundation charter of Prague University, issued by Charles IV on 7 April 1348. The second copy of the foundation charter with an attached wax seal, intended for the university's chancellor, Archbishop Ernest of Pardubice.

The seal of the Prague University community with which from the 14th century until today Charles University has marked its diplomas and awards granted. The seal depicts a kneeling Charles IV with a founding charter of Prague University entrusting higher learning to the protection of Prince Wenceslas, the patron of the Czech Lands and also of the university.

as extra fees for certificates and diplomas. The universal language of the learned in the medieval period and also in the early modern period was Latin. All university teaching took place in this language and, precisely thanks to this universal language, students, masters and doctors were able to move from one Western university to another and thus participate in the creation of an international community. A university was supposed to create an independent spiritual space, protected from pressures on the part of secular power. The freedom of academic ground was connected to this. Members of police and criminal investigation bodies were not permitted to enter the premises of university buildings in order to interfere officially there of their own volition. In matters of criminal law the members of the university community were not subject to city courts or any other courts. On the contrary, the task of external secular power was to provide university general studies with both material provision and legal protection. However, the historical reality shows that on more than one occasion universities had to back down and make concessions at the expense of academic freedoms, spiritual life and the direction of studies.

The doctors who created the content and system of study were associated in colleges according to individual faculties. The buildings of the colleges became spaces for teaching and research, but also for accommodation, offices of the university's self-governing administration and assemblies of members of the academic community. It must be added that medieval doctors and masters lived in celibacy in the college houses. The university system was formed of faculties headed by deans. The highest administrative function with accompanying powers was held by the rector, elected by the university community as a rule for a year. The symbols of power (insignia), which included the rector's sceptre, the university seal, the rector's seal and the key to the treasury containing valuables, were handed over to the new rector by his predecessor during the ceremonial induction into office. Deans of faculties also held the seals and sceptres of their faculties. In the beginnings of Prague University it was not possible to realize fully the statutory form of the university system that arose in Oxford and Cambridge. Funds and also appropriate buildings were lacking, even though in the founding charter Charles offered 'excellent estates' and 'kingly gifts'.

At first Prague Archbishop Ernest of Pardubice, who was university chancellor by virtue of his office, provided help. In 1352 he imposed a special tax on the clerics of the Prague archdiocese, as a result of which the university acquired several villages and courts. The profits from this tax on the village serfs, together with funds from

Doctor and pupil depicted in the Jena codex from the period around 1500. The ceremonial dress, a pleated sleeveless long gown (tapert) and biretta, was prescribed by a dress code to ensure that doctors were dressed smartly and distinctly so that the dignity of their position was made clear, as stated in the inscription.

A master of liberal arts teaching pupils. The initial P in a manuscript from the turn of the 14th and 15th centuries.

donor foundations, enabled the university to pay the salaries of teachers and other essential expenses. Thanks to the generosity of the archbishop, the castle chapter of St. Vitus Cathedral, monastic convents and the Tyn parish school in Prague's Old Town, the corporations of higher learning found premises in traditional institutions of learning and education. For the purpose of ceremonial assemblies of the university community, the archbishop opened up St. Vitus Cathedral and the refectory hall in the Archbishop's Court in the Lesser Town.

As the number of teachers and pupils increased in Prague, this provisional accommodation ceased to be sufficient. Several monasteries, from which teachers were also recruited, provided substantial help. For instance, in 1383 the general studies course (including its teachers) of the Dominican monastery of Saint Clement in the Old Town opposite Charles Bridge (on the site of the later Klementinum) was incorporated into the university community. Similarly, the general studies taught at the Monastery of Augustinian Eremites at Saint Thomas in the Lesser Town and also the *studium generale* at the Monastery of the Minorites in the Old Town were incorporated into the university.

It was only after 18 years, in 1366, that Charles IV himself dedicated substantial funds for the acquisition of buildings. During this period that Prague University existed in a provisional state, competing institutions of higher learning were founded:

Dominican Jakub of Prague at a writing desk, depicted with an owl as the symbol of wisdom in antiquity.
Gradual of Master Wenceslas (Václav), a professor
at Prague University, from the period around 1400.

in Krakow in 1364 and in Vienna one year later. This increased Prague University's need for a 'Great College' as a representative central building. The ruler acquired for the university a building that had once belonged to a Jew named Lazarus, which was probably situated in the busy urban area where the Old Town bordered the Jewish Town, in today's Široká (Broad) Street. Neither this building, nor that of the college of the arts faculty founded seven years earlier, has survived. Over the many years of rebuilding in Prague the buildings of 17 other masters and students colleges and bursae (masters' quarters, at which students were accommodated), which we know were founded during the pre-Hussite expansion of higher learning in the last third of the 14th century and the beginning of the 15th century, have also disappeared.

Great College, also known as Charles College and founded by the ruler in 1366 during the university's blossoming, was intended as a place for 12 masters of the faculty of the seven liberal arts – masters of arts who were also capable of teaching theology – to live and work. The university statute from 1360 did not stipulate that students of theology, medicine or law first had to undergo a period of study at the Faculty of Liberal Arts. However, in practice it was hardly imaginable for a student not to have a preparation in the seven liberal arts, which provided the bases of higher learning by acquainting him with philosophy and scholastic methods and giving him a cultural and moral overview. Teaching at the liberal arts faculty was divided into two branches: the *trivium*, which comprised grammar, rhetoric and dialectics, and the *quadrivium*, which comprised arithmetic, geometry, astronomy and the musical arts. The faculty, which had the largest number of masters and also students, grew along with the development of the entire Prague higher learning from the 1360s.

Charles IV's son and successor Wenceslas IV donated two colleges to the university in 1381. The first, bearing his name – King Wenceslas College or Imperial College – was located at New Market (today Fruit Market – Ovocný Trh). The building with a tower and garden was retained by the university even through the Hussite wars. It only sold the building in a public auction in 1757 on condition that the building retained its name in the future. The second college of Wenceslas's gift was the building today known as Karolinum. Finally, 38 years after the university's foundation, it received a dignified and spacious central premises at New Market. The building had originally been constructed for himself and his descendants by Johlin (Jan) Rotlev (originally Rotlöw – meaning Red Lion), whose coat-of-arms depicted a red lion ascending. Rotlev was the master of the king's mint, banker to the king and one of the richest traders in precious metals in the kingdom, and it is no surprise that, when Wenceslas IV wanted to provide the university with dignified premises, his choice in 1383 fell precisely on Rotlev's palace. The residence was built after 1360 by joining several houses in a block of houses on the corner of New Market and Kamzíková and Železná streets. Some remains of the older building are preserved today in the cellars of Karolinum and also on the building's ground floor. The residence had two storeys and the ceremonial rooms took up the first floor. Wenceslas IV possibly acquired the building from Jan Rotlev's son Martin in exchange for Koloděje Castle with its surrounding estate, or possibly – as a legend relates – as a fine for the unwarranted drawing of weapons at court. Over three years he had the palace altered to enable Charles College (Karolinum) to move into the building. The college's existing cramped premises were no longer sufficient to satisfy the level of interest in study, in particular at the Faculty of Liberal Arts. The university was to gain a representative building meeting all its requirements.

The ingenious reconstruction primarily changed Rotlev's palace in a functional way. The imposing palace, built with a view to family privacy, could not fulfil the role of premises appropriate for a busy university. The design for the reconstruction was based on the tried-and-tested architecture used in monasteries: a closed quadrangle surrounding an internal courtyard, linked by a system of long corridors in the manner of cloisters. This was the way in which, for instance, the new buildings of the colleges in Oxford and Bologna were constructed. The Sorbonne in Paris and Prague's Karolinum, whose ground plans were predetermined by constricted city land plots and a core of town houses, attempted to get as close as possible to this prototype in order to include within their walls not only the masters' quarters, but also lecture rooms, assembly halls and administrative facilities, including the treasury and the university's own prison (*carcer*). In the gradual reconstruction the architect focused first on the existing representative building: he had unnecessary bowers removed and in their place had corridors built enabling an entrance to separate rooms. On the upper floors wooden courtyard balconies, and in some cases galleries supported on stone pillars, served this connecting purpose.

Wenceslas IV's attempt to create some kind of university 'campus' around New Market cannot be overlooked. Around the year 1383 he had his own temporary residence, the so-called King's Court, built in the near vicinity of the neighbouring Imperial College. Most probably from 1391 onwards the U Černé růže (Black Rose) house by the moat (Příkopy) on the New Town side also belonged to these premises. The area of the Old Town's moat bulwarks, previously used sparingly for building, provided valuable land plots. It had been the wish of the Luxembourg founders to join Prague's several towns in one metropolis, but this only came about permanently four centuries later. The College of the Bohemian Nation (Czech College) had already been established before 1391 near Wenceslas College at New Market in the Old Town. The college's name bears witness to the ongoing mutual disputes between the corporations of the so-called university nations.

Prague University underwent its greatest period of growth in the 1370s and 1380s, when according to estimates it had a total of between 2,500 and 3,000 masters, doctors and students. At the beginning of the 15th century, when the university was facing competition from other newly founded central European universities, it had more than a thousand students. The estimated total number of inhabitants of the four Prague towns, which Charles IV wanted to join together, improve and extend into a metropolis of the Holy Roman Empire of the West European type, was around 40,000.

By his generous donations to the university King Wenceslas IV was undoubtedly expressing his appreciation for the political support that its masters and doctors had

The Romanesque hall in the cellar of house number 16 in the Old Town with dimensions 5 × 6 m, vaulted by a four-section ceiling of cross vaults, supported by a central column, was a part of the College of All Souls, apparently as a ground-floor assembly place of masters and students of the Faculty of Liberal Arts.

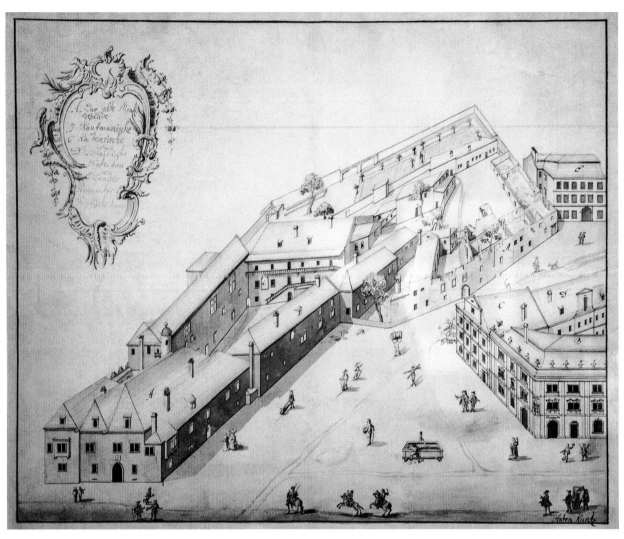

ANTONÍN KUNTZ: **Area of university colleges around Ovocný trh (Fruit Market) in a plan for the reconstruction of the Prague mint from 1740.**

given him in political disputes within the empire. He became imperial ruler after his father's death in 1378 at the age of 18 at a time of growing aggression on the part of domestic opposition noblemen toward a weakened sovereign power.

In contrast to university teachers, students intervened in politics only in extreme situations. On the other hand, they had a strong influence on the everyday life of medieval Prague outside of the enclosed college premises. They mostly came to university earlier than is the case today, between the ages of 16 and 18, immature in thought and without any great experience of life. In general they started their studies at the Faculty of Liberal Arts, which was the largest faculty. A basic condition for acceptance at the university was a knowledge of Latin, the universal language of the educated, which enabled travel for the purpose of gaining knowledge and education. These itinerant students (known as vagrants from the Latin *vagare*) brought their lifestyle, customs in food, clothes, entertainment, songs, verses and music, as well as their opinions on social organization, from one university to another. They cited their youth as an excuse for their noisiness and rumbustious behaviour; their privileged status as members of the academic community gave them protection in

Books represented a considerable amount of wealth. During their travels for the purpose of education students and teachers took great care of them and even had a special binding for the purpose of travel. The travel binding depicted in this late Gothic statue in Strahov Monastery has the attributes of St. John the Evangelist, who among other things is the protector of writers and all those who participate in the publishing of books.

the case of behavioural excesses. They did not spare irony and satire toward the townsfolk and the serfs who had to earn their families' daily bread by the sweat of their brow. Students were criticized by moral preachers who reproached them for spending their time in taverns and corrupting decent Christians with their boisterous lifestyle. In the words of one of the student drinking songs: *We don't care about learning, it's pleasant to know nothing, all we care about in our youth is where to find as much pleasure as we can.* Offences committed by students against public order were not within the jurisdiction of the city courts, but that of the university authorities, who could hand out fines and also corporal punishment. Entry to the exceptional position of student – member of the academic community – was accompanied by a satirical, somewhat cruel, initiation ritual called 'beánie', in which older students accepted a newcomer amongst themselves.

The social festivals of the town were governed by the liturgical calendar and students joined in them enthusiastically along with the other inhabitants of Prague, primarily during the Lent processions and games. However, they traditionally regarded some festivals, such as the 'festival of fools', as their own and organized them themselves. The essence of these festivals was the 'world turned upside down', a parody of serious church services and symbols. On certain days this activity of the students was tolerated, primarily on the festival of their fictive holy protectors, the Innocents of Bethlehem. The festival started with the election of the 'pupil's bishop', who received a gown, crosier, mitre and temporary powers. The procession with the fake bishop seated backwards on a donkey – that is, facing its tail – headed toward the church, where the festival culminated in a 'donkey's mass', a parody of a religious service. Jan Hus (John Huss), who left a personal account of the course of such a farce, described how the donkey was led inside the church, fed and inebriated with beer. A part of the entertainment was the pupil's carol during which contributions were collected from the audience. The students took a similarly active role on the eve of the festival of Saint Nicholas, primarily in the accompanying mounted escort 'the knights of Saint Nicholas'. Saint Nicholas is, among other things, the patron saint of children and pupils, and a wild ride on decorated horses in his honour was a welcome opportunity for the students to compensate for the hours, days and weeks spent in listening to lectures, engaging in academic disputation, preparing for exams, writing notes and memorizing out loud. Repeating out loud and rigid committing to memory was still the main teaching method in the medieval period. Master Claretus de Solencia (Bartoloměj z Chlumce), one of the first graduates of Prague higher learning, spent years of diligent work in 'bashing Latin expressions into the heads' of Czech students and in drilling Czech expressions into foreign students. His ency-clopedic Latin-Czech dictionaries, which contained around 10,000 Czech words and their Latin equivalents, are written in rhyme with a view to learning them by heart.

Of course learned disputations and disputes connected with efforts at reform-ing the church and with a humanist conception of the world gradually seeped into private classrooms and common university assemblies. In Prague's towns, which had a dense structure of church institutions, the autonomous university community did not stand aside from the historical process of the deepening of individual spiri-tual life or the social conflicts of the period. In particular the young generation of doctors and masters, enriched by reformist opinions, tried to bring these reformist ideas to life, and to do so with the support of secular power. Wenceslas IV and a group of his courtiers, associated in the Brotherhood of the Hammer and Hoop, dedicated substantial funds to the building between 1382 and 1393 of the Corpus Christi Chapel, a architectural gem with a central polygonal tower, in the middle of the New Town Market (today Karlovo náměstí). The place of construction was already earlier a sacred location: since the middle of the 14th century the imperial and Czech holy relics had been displayed here annually to pilgrims. From the year 1403 this chapel belonged to the university college of the Bohemian nation and played a significant role in the later history of Prague. It was closed by Joseph II in 1784 and subsequently knocked down (1791). The preaching post at the Corpus Christi Chapel became one of the platforms of the Czech reformation: in their preaching here university masters had the opportunity to present reformist ideas to a wider public in such a way as to deepen the religious experience of individuals. This found a significant response at a time of uncertainty, plagues and social crises.

The second and better known platform of the reformation was the chapel in the Old Town known as the Bethlehem Chapel, which was dedicated to the Holy Innocents of Bethlehem (whose feast was celebrated on December 28 according to the church calendar), who served as the patron saints of students. In 1391 Hanuš of Milheim, a courtier of Wenceslas IV, gave substantial funds for the building of this chapel and Václav Kříž, a rich Old Town councillor and merchant, donated the land plot. The founding charter directly stated the requirements that the chapel's priest should preach freely in the Czech language every day in the morning and at

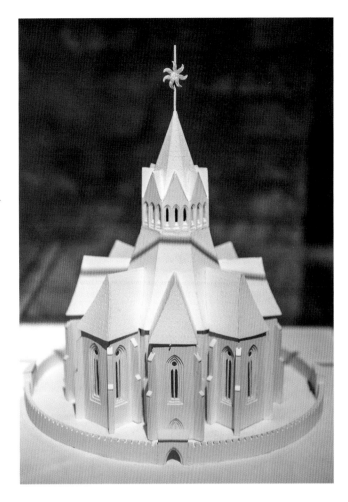

Model of Corpus Christi Chapel, built in the years 1382–1393 to a central polygonal plan. The chapel stood in the middle of Cattle Market (today Karlovo náměstí – Charles Square). Every year at Easter the holiest relics acquired by Charles IV were shown to pilgrims here and on the anniversary of his death a mourning procession made its way here. From 1403 the chapel belonged to the university college of the Czech nation. It served as an assembly place and also for the declaration of important decrees. In 1437 the masters published the Basel Compacts here. The most important members of the university community also found their last resting place here. The last of them to be buried here in 1622, before the chapel was taken over by the Jesuits, was Rector Jan Campanus Vodňanský, a tragic figure of the defeated revolt of the estates (1618–1620).

noon, that he should himself live in the chapel, and that he should use gifts from the pious for the upkeep of the chapel and also for the sustenance of poor students. The Bethlehem Chapel has established itself in the national consciousness as the workplace of Master Jan Hus, one of the chapel's administrators. Hus presented his opinions here and attracted great interest from the public.

In 1406 the generous merchant Kříž also donated to the university the adjoining house, which was connected by an alleyway with Dominikánská (today Husova) Street. A college called Nazareth was founded here, and Jan Hus also became administrator of this college. It became commonly known as Preacher's College, which tells us a lot. Kříž was a long-term benefactor of the university in the Old Town. A subtext of this activity on the part of benefactors on the threshold of the Hussite era can be found in the burgeoning disputes between the corporations of the various university nations. This was not only a case of the foundation of the College of the Czech Nation and of the university pulpits. An increasing number of foundations of wealthy Prague citizens provided support for the university corporation of the Bohemian (Czech) nation (Nacio Bohemorum): these financed the purchase of houses, which were then converted into colleges. The corporation of the Polish nation also made efforts to establish its own college. In 1397 Václav Kříž had already rented rooms for 12 students from Lithuania (from the corporation of the Polish university nation) at the Cistercian monastery in Bartolomějská Street. This was initially called the Jerusalem College. In 1413 the college, with the new name of Jadwiga's College

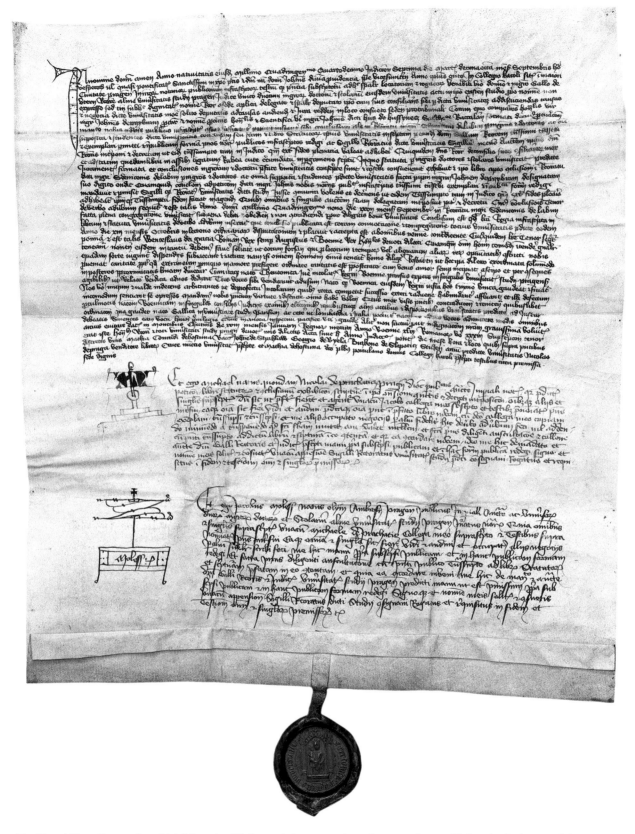

The Kutná Hora Decree, by which Wencelas IV changed the proportion of votes at Prague University in favour of the Bohemian university nation. After the decree the Bohemian nation had a predominance of three votes compared to one for each of the foreign nations. The decree was declared on 18 January 1409 in Kutná Hora and influenced the fate of Prague and of the university itself for many years to come.

(College of Lithuanian Queen Jadwiga), was moved to the new university premises then being established at Fruit Market in the neighbourhood of the College of the Bohemian Nation and of Wenceslas's College.

The mass departure of a substantial part of the students of the liberal arts, theological and medical faculties following the issuing of the Kutná Hora Decree in 1409 did not have its causes in nationalism as we know it in the modern period, even though the spread of national languages into writing certainly played a role here. The impulse for disputes and quarrels in the university community was given by the previous long-term disagreements among the four national corporations regarding decisions on the foundation of colleges and the sharing of material gifts and funds, including the remuneration of masters and doctors. From the beginning of the 14th century six new universities were founded within the catchment area of Prague University, and Polish, Saxon and Bavarian students were able to choose a university closer to their home. If we leave to one side the usual personal disagreements among doctors and masters, in Prague there were also disputes regarding inclination to the reform movement and the stance of church representatives toward the issue of the papal schism. Representatives of the Czech university nation requested greater influence on the running of the university and expected support from King Wenceslas IV, whose side they had taken in his quarrel with the archbishop. In addition, on the whole they belonged to the reform movement. Master Jan Hus himself, as future rector, participated zealously in this program of the majority of the Bohemian university nation. In 1409 King Wenceslas IV changed the proportion of votes in decisions on the running of faculties and colleges (with the exception of the Law Faculty) to the advantage of the Bohemian nation. In protest a large number of doctors and masters, and along with them their students, decided to leave Prague University: around 700 people left Prague at that time. This event had a lasting influence on the university's further development and in particular on Prague's cultural and spiritual life. The departure of teachers and students as a result of an intervention by state power in the university's status, together with other factors, weakened the state of higher learning in the Kingdom of Bohemia so much that on the threshold of the Hussite period the university's three faculties had been reduced to one faculty, that of liberal arts, and the university was subject to secular power in a kingdom of estates. The Kutná Hora Decree is regarded as one of the milestones in the process by which higher learning in Prague lost its privileged position in central Europe and became one of the regional locations of a *studium generale*.

The Hussite era fundamentally changed the university's entire statutory system and thus its continuous connection with the life of Prague and the entire Bohemian society. Even after the defeat of the Hussite field armies, the university remained associated with clerical dissent and with the power-political program that established a kingdom of estates with two peoples. The university remained in isolation from a hostile Europe, which regarded the inhabitants of Bohemia as heretics and apostates from the true faith. It is hardly possible to imagine that a foreign student from Catholic Europe would submit to the compulsory oath contained in the Basel Compacts, which came into force in 1436. The compacts represented a compromise agreement between the Catholic Church and the Bohemian Utraquists (Calixtinists). The masters of Prague University participated in the formulation of the compacts and they regarded the document containing them as an achievement of reformist efforts.

Master Jan Hus (John Huss), rector of Prague University from 1409 to 1410, who was burned at the stake as a heretic on 6 July 1415 in Constance, after he failed to persuade the church council of the correctness of his theses. Jena codex from the period around 1500.

From the year 1462, students had to take the compulsory oath, which was inscribed in stone in the Corpus Christi Chapel. This meant that learning at Charles University became closed off from the outside world for many decades both in terms of religious confession and of nationality. The function of university chancellor, which had been held since its foundation by the archbishop of Prague, was transferred to the rector.

In political terms the weakened university with only one faculty, that of liberal arts, maintained relations with representatives of the estates and lent them support for the entire period prior to the Battle of White Mountain (1620). For instance, the university masters prepared important political documents. As an Utraquist educational institution the university took under its roof the Utraquist church administration, the so-called Lower Consistory. Evidence of the close links between the estates and the university is also provided by the fact that representatives of the Bohemian estates set out for Prague Castle for the defenestration of the lords regent in 1618 directly after holding a meeting at Karolinum. The university's rector Jan Jesenský (Jesenius/Jessenius) provided diplomatic services to the leaders of the Bohemian Revolt, the uprising of the estates from 1618 to 1620, and paid for this with his own head at the place of execution outside the town hall on the Old Town Square in 1621.

During the long pre-White Mountain period, when the university was in thrall to politicians of the Bohemian Estates, its material wealth decreased substantially. Nevertheless, it fulfilled an indispensable role for society: it educated a new Utraquist intelligentsia, as well as churchmen and municipal school teachers. We register the first large donor gifts to the university for the building of student colleges at the end of the 1430s. In 1438 Jan Reček, installed by the emperor as burgermeister (mayor) of the Old Town, founded Reček College, also known as Virgin Mary College, for this purpose. The new college's name reveals that it was intended to strengthen the moderate reformist wing of the Utraquist movement, which wanted to retain respect toward the Virgin Mary. The college's students were initially accommodated at the College of the Bohemian Nation, but after 1439 they moved to a courtyard with a tower close to the Church of St. Stephen in the Wall. In the post-White Mountain period the Jesuits converted the college into a brewery.

Matěj Louda z Chlumčan, a one-time commander of Tabor and an adherent of the more radical wing of the Utraquists, also contributed to the education of future Utraquist intellectuals, in particular priests, of whom there was a desperate shortage. In 1439 he purchased a house near Nazareth College. He had the house converted into a college for poor students called the College of the Apostles (or Laudon College) and he also provided a library. This college must have had a good level because among its alumni was the son of King George (Jiří) of Poděbrady. This college, like Nazareth College, was administered by the preachers of the Bethlehem Chapel. The university's premises were further extended in 1590 by a legacy from Mayor Václav Krocín z Drahobejle. His house in Betlémská Street near the parish church of Saint Andrew was converted into the Poor Students College, also known as Saint Andrew's College. If we evaluate this long era, which we can designate as the Hussite period in the university's history, we are inclined to recall the old thesis about the deception of history. The Prague doctors and university masters were ahead of their time in propagating the avant-garde ideas of the reformation – ideas aimed at improving human relations and increasing awareness of spiritual values and responsibility. Their efforts were premature, as society at the turn of the 14th and 15th centuries was not ripe for changes of greater extent. On the one hand, they failed to reckon with latent power and economic interests; with the efforts of the oligarchs to gain control of church and royal property by military means. On the other hand, they did not reckon with the potential reaction of the fanatical mob to a radical eschatological vision offering wealth and social conciliation.

If we leave to one side the disputes regarding religious confession and the estates, the 16th century also introduced an entirely new concept of education into university lecture halls, and not only in Prague. Primarily as a result of book printing, a universal humanist interest in acquiring knowledge of the world began to spread. Suddenly universities were no longer capable of keeping pace with the sum of education and learning, over which they had previously had a virtual monopoly. Printed learned literature, issued at home and abroad, substantially enriched the medieval manuscript libraries of colleges and private libraries. Some of the book collections from that time have been preserved to this day at the National Library in Prague's Klementinum. The medieval archetype of scholastic education was fundamentally changed. Humanist reason was based on the disciplines of natural science and it acknowledged mathematical descriptions as having the character of answers about the

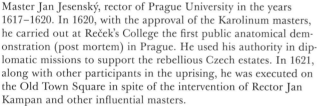

Master Jan Jesenský, rector of Prague University in the years 1617–1620. In 1620, with the approval of the Karolinum masters, he carried out at Reček's College the first public anatomical demonstration (post mortem) in Prague. He used his authority in diplomatic missions to support the rebellious Czech estates. In 1621, along with other participants in the uprising, he was executed on the Old Town Square in spite of the intervention of Rector Jan Kampan and other influential masters.

Master Tadeáš Hájek of Hájek, an important natural scientist of Rudolphinian Prague. The doctor, botanist and astronomer had to leave the university, similarly to some other masters, when he married. The university did not abolish compulsory celibacy until 1612.

actual nature of the world. This approach applied already in the case of Copernicus, made a breakthrough in Newton's works and was fully developed in the science of the 17th to 19th centuries, during which time a revolutionary modern-age classification of sciences occurred. Even in the humanist period old university programs continued to have a holistic approach to education; scholars at that time were in their way polymaths. Knowledge from the expanding spectrum of scientific disciplines could be acquired rather in supplementary lessons than in the compulsory program.

The situation was especially difficult for the one-faculty (liberal arts) university of Prague. After the Hussite wars the three other original faculties (law, medicine and theology) were not re-established, even though there are some indications that some individuals continued in the teaching of the foundations of medicine, which the arts faculty included in its program. As the university's significance declined, so its buildings also began to decay. Two classrooms, one of them a 'winter' room with heating, and an office on Karolinum's first floor were sufficient for the regular operation of the faculty. In 1538, when the students held a theatrical performance for the public in Karolinum's courtyard, the balconies on the first and second floors, from which the audience normally watched, almost collapsed. There were no funds for repairs and so theatre performances were discontinued here. In the final decades of the 16th century lectures on law were successfully revived, even though there was no independent law faculty.

Modern-age research deepening the knowledge of specialist sciences was at first rather the private hobby of broadly educated masters: for instance, the astronomical research of Tadeáš Hájek, who in the second half of the 16th century connected a group of university teachers together with a group of learned men from the imperial court in the centre of Prague. We can also mention Master Adam Zalužanský, who carried out breakthrough work in the field of plant physiology and morphology outside the program of teaching, as well as the astronomical studies of Jan Jesenský or one of the last Bohemian polymaths Jan Marcus Marci. Another important figure of the Renaissance university was Martin Bacháček of Nauměřice, who was its rector at the turn of the 16th and 17th centuries and carried out studies in mathematics, astronomy, cosmography and geography. He studied at a number of Protestant universities, which was made possible by the European Reformation. The circle of Catholic universities was substantially extended by the addition of new universities that were different both in terms of confession and of power interests. After his return to Prague, Martin Bacháček assembled a group of learned men who were open to new scientific knowledge and methods. Rudolphinian Prague was not only marked by an elevated cultural atmosphere. The university also gained a significant boost from the presence of foreign humanist scholars at Rudolph's court, among them Tycho Brahe and other astronomers, including Johannes Kepler, who was accommodated by the university at the College of Wenceslas IV. We should also note the success achieved by the university in spreading general education during Martin Bacháček's term as rector. The number of Latin (grammar) schools under university supervision increased. At the time almost all free royal towns had such a grammar school, which prepared students for university study, as did many subject towns and even some small towns and, exceptionally, villages. At the beginning of the 17th century there were 125 such schools under the administration of Prague University's rector. In comparison with West European countries this was one of the densest school networks anywhere.

Alongside universities with the right to offer general studies and award academic titles, the period from the 16th century onwards saw the foundation of specialist state and private places of higher learning known as *academia*. In connection with the growth of manufacturing these academies concentrated their attention more and more on scientific and technical fields of study. Some individual university teachers were also inclined toward specializations that could be used in manufacturing processes. Such teachers felt a lack of new trends in research at the universities. This signalled the start of the formation of a new university system. From the 17th century onwards individuals interested in new trends joined together in learned societies, which were also called academies. This was the onset of a new era in the development of European higher learning that saw an increase in theoretical research that was linked to applied research. At a time of developing ideas connected to the Reformation in Europe traditional Bohemian Utraquistism was becoming somewhat outdated. In the middle of the 16th century more than 80 percent of the country's population avowed a non-Catholic faith. This also applied to the Utraquist Consistory and the university connected with it. The Catholic Habsburg rulers in a country with a predominantly Utraquist population were compelled to seek compromise and also to take into account Reformation Europe at a time when power was divided in accordance with confessional ideologies. When Ferdinand I ascended to the Bohemian throne (1526), he took an oath to comply with the Basel Compacts from 1436 and this meant that he had his hands tied in supporting Catholicism. It was not until 1561 that he succeeded in renewing an archbishopric in the royal city of Prague. He would also have liked to have seen Prague's university become Catholic. However, the university resisted this, as it had strong support in the ranks of the Bohemian estates, especially in the estate of town burghers led by representatives of the towns of Prague. The university even took part in the uprising of the Bohemian Estates in 1545.

After the defeat of this uprising the Habsburg ruler choose a different tactic for the re-establishment of Catholicism: he found support in the newly founded and intellectually dynamic order of the Jesuits. From the beginning the Jesuits focused both on Latin grammar schools and on university-level general education, but also on the mutual interconnection between these two levels. On 18 April 1556 Ferdinand I summoned from Rome 12 members of the Society of Jesus – the Jesuits. He settled them at the Church of St. Clement in the Old Town near Charles Bridge in the premises of the former Dominican Monastery. In 1562 the Jesuits established the College of St. Clement (Klementinum) here. At first the *Academia Pragensis Societatis Jesu*, as it was officially known, did not have the status of a university. It attained this status more or less formally in 1616, even though it had awarded titles already before this. It was headed by a rector appointed by a representative of the Jesuit order and was not divided into faculties. It was not, therefore, an autonomous corporation, as universities from their medieval beginnings were. In other countries also Jesuit academies were not connected in a statutory way to the system of medieval universities.

The Jesuits were more successful in making use of the humanist changes in the content and methods of teaching and also in making a firmer and more effective link between grammar school and university teaching than the Utraquist university under Rector Baháček, even though Baháček and his academic body also attempted to achieve these aims. At Jesuit colleges attendance at a five-year grammar school provided a basis and preparation for a three-year university course in philosophy. After graduating from this, students could then register for a further two-year university study of theology. On the whole the Jesuits in Prague came from the German-speaking parts of the empire and were chosen for both their academic knowledge and their teaching skills.

Prague University gained a capable competitor. Up until the Bohemian Revolt in 1618, when the Jesuits left Prague, a one-faculty Utraquist Charles University competed with the Jesuit Academy at Klementinum. This dual system continued when the Jesuits returned following the defeat of the uprising of the estates. The Counter-Reformation had a strong impact on the fate of Prague University. For many years the future form of the university was the subject of disputes between the emperor, the Jesuits and Prague Archbishop Ernest of Harrach. In 1654 the two institutes of higher learning – Karolinum and Klementinum – were merged into one university, renamed the Charles-Ferdinand University. The very name of the university itself – *Caesarea regia Universitas Carolo-Ferdinandae Pragensis*, which the university bore up until 1882 (its division into Czech and German parts) – makes clear the supervision that the emperor arrogated for himself and also the fact that the state took on the university's management. This had far-reaching consequences for the statutory organization of higher learning in Prague. The university once again had four faculties. The two spiritual faculties – philosophical and theological – were located at Klementinum and taught there by the Jesuits. The other two – medicine and jurisprudence – remained at Karolinum and were taught there by secular professors. All students and also professors had to be Catholics and already from 1650 onwards students at their graduation had to swear an oath to the Immaculate Conception of the Virgin Mary.

When evaluating the further development of the renewed four-faculty Prague University, created in 1654 by combining the institutes of higher education at Karolinum and Klementinum, we must be aware that it underwent the necessary changes of European universities, but was also subject to the disputes of domestic parties. The very task of education, which originally consisted in the need to improve human morality and spread scientific knowledge, also changed. A more pragmatic approach gained ground in connection with the needs of practical skills in the context of innovations taking place in civilization. The long-term dilemma concerning the statutory form of universities and academies, in which the state interfered more and more in the early modern era, was also reflected in the development of university education. At first, at the turn of the 18th and 19th centuries, this interference by the state, within the framework of clerical political power, took the form of promoting

Academia Triumphans. This is the name of the symbolic tableau in which the engraver celebrated the foundation of the re-Catholicized Charles-Ferdinand University in 1654, created by the merger of the Jesuit Academy and the originally Utraquist Charles University. The university, depicted in the form of a victorious female warrior, raises a shield with a picture of the university's seal, but also stabs the defeated Protestant past of the university with a spear. Frontispiece of a book by M. Volckmann, *Gloria Universitatis Carolo-Ferdinandae*, published in 1672 in Prague.

confessional tolerance. However, this state interference also had tragic consequences in the form of a spread of nationalism. From the second half of the 17th century and during the 18th century the state had an increasing interest in the results of study in new fields such as the state-science, mercantilism and physiocrasy. The syllabus of the Law Faculty was extended to include the field of statistics, which at that time was part of a wider field of study called state-science. The need for professional experts and technical specifications forced the state to support, according to its needs, various specialized branches of education – industrial, technical, military – but also to subject the universities to the state's interests without paying any great consideration to their long corporative traditions and freedoms.

During the last quarter of the 18th century and the beginning of the 19th century there was a unification and bureaucratization of European universities generally, which limited the freedom of movement of both students and pedagogues. Teaching and research at universities was also regulated according to the notions of government councils. Existing disciplines were supplemented by new subjects needed from the point of view of the organization of society. In the Habsburg monarchy reformist efforts were often also initiated by professors themselves: at Prague University this happened mainly in the 1780s and 1790s. These two decades saw the foundation, with state support, of a botanical garden and a chemical laboratory at the Faculty of Medicine. Students were also now required to spend time at clinics, which enabled practical instruction. A specialized collection was established at the Philosophy Faculty: this consisted of a public cabinet of natural phenomena and also a cabinet of physical phenomena, which was acquired by the Polytechnic Institute in 1815 following its separation from the university. The observatory at Klementinum was modernized and in 1775 the meteorological station was the first in Europe to begin regular meteorological measurements, a practice that has continued to this day. The Philosophy Faculty, previously the Faculty of Liberal Arts, changed not only its name, but also its program of study. It was precisely this faculty that extended both the spectrum of specialized scientific disciplines and also the breadth of the program of studies. The faculty, which was previously rather focused on preparatory general studies, accepted into its program the subjects of philosophy, history, literature, philology, mathematics, geography and physics, as well as technical and natural scientific specialisms. The magnificently built Klementinum complex also provided appropriate premises for this expansion of disciplines. For a certain period Klementinum was home not only to the polytechnic, but also to an academy of fine arts.

The Jesuits continued to teach at the two spiritual faculties located at Klementinum – the philosophical and theological faculties – in accordance with their own statutory rules up until the order's abolition in 1773. Secular professors taught at the two much more modest secular faculties at Karolinum – the juridical and medical faculties. The material situation at the two locations was substantially different and the two secular faculties were much worse equipped and dilapidated. Already at the time of their arrival in Prague in the mid-16th century the Jesuits had reckoned with the construction of a new complex at Klementinum. Before 1618 they purchased or were donated 32 town houses, seven courts and two extensive gardens. During the Counter-Reformation period after the Battle of White Mountain, when the Jesuits already reckoned with their inclusion in the combined Charles-Ferdinand University, in 1653 they embarked on a process of construction that lasted until the

Display cabinet with minerals from the Mathematical Museum at Klementinum depicted in a volume by Johann Kisling *Compendium physicae experimentalis ...*, 1747.
The systematic collection of minerals was the pride of the Klementinum Museum, opened on the occasion of the coronation of Charles VI in 1723. In addition to minerals, scientific instruments, books, graphics and herbariums, the Jesuits also collected various exotic objects and clock mechanisms here.

mid-18th century. Over a period of about 100 years a number of famous architects and important Baroque painters and sculptors (Domenico Orsi, Kilian Ignaz Dientzenhofer, František Maxmilián Kaňka and others) worked here. Klementinum provided education in the fields of the arts, natural sciences and technical disciplines. For the purposes of teaching the Jesuits collected rare natural scientific samples and technical aids which were later incorporated into the collections of the Klementinum Museum of Mathematics, founded in 1722 as the first public museum in central Europe. The preserved instruments from the pre-White Mountain period give us an idea in particular of the interests of those learned men teaching at grammar schools and in the three-year philosophy course. The instruments served as teaching aids in mathematics, physics, mechanics, astronomy and mineralogy.

While the Klementinum university complex grew during the Baroque period, the Karolinum medieval university complex went into long-term decline. There were no funds even for maintenance, let alone for reconstruction. At the end of the 17th century the northern and eastern buildings at Karolinum were uninhabitable. The ground floor, which had lost its arcades when they were walled up in the course of Renaissance alterations, was used for storage space, tradesmen's workshops and accommodation, shops and a tavern, from all of which the university received a regular rent. When subsequently a part of the eastern wing collapsed and the courtyard balconies were in danger of falling down, the rector and the professors of the medical and jurisprudence faculties decided in 1714 that they would not teach in the life-threatening ruins. Teaching was moved to Wenceslas College, which was slightly less dilapidated, and disputations and graduation ceremonies to the Tyn Church (in the nearby Old Town Square). The professors requested a state commission to have Karolinum repaired because 'nowhere else in the world does study take place in such a bad building'. They requested premises for the university and for the education of medical doctors. The alterations were entrusted to architect F. M. Kaňka, who saved the premises at the last moment. He did away with the medieval accommodation quarters of masters and students and modernized the buildings to provide everything needed for teaching and university administration: seven lecture halls, including the Aula Magna, offices and a library. Nevertheless, in contrast to Klementinum, the limits of public finances restricted architect Kaňka to the most essential repairs at Karolinum and precluded modernization. Medical doctor Jan Theobald Held later recalled his time spent in one of the lecture halls: *the lecture hall of pharmaceutical chemistry was a real barn, where we were tortured not only by the deadly air, but also by coal gases and smoke arising from the preparation of chemical substances. During the winter in seven to nine of the lecture halls there ink froze in the ink pots and our toenails froze in our boots...*

Newly introduced specialisms in particular encountered problems of lack of space. Meanwhile, the modernization of teaching was unthinkable without laboratories. The worst situation was probably at the Faculty of Medicine, where clinics became an essential part of teaching and research. We should recall that from the Middle Ages surgery was not a subject of teaching at medical faculties, but rather an independent trade. Since its re-establishment in the second half of the 17th century the Faculty of Medicine had worked with health and charitable institutions in Prague in organizing demonstrations of anatomy. Demonstrations of clinical practice took place in Prague hospitals (Hospital of the Merciful Brothers and the Italian (Vlašský) Hospital) as well as in prisons and in the apartments of patients. At the end of the 18th century charitable foundations financed the establishment of maternity wards for foundlings at the St. Appolinaire Hospital (1789) and the General Hospital (1790), at which establishments a limited number of beds were maintained from study funds. Before the middle of the 19th century medical students also spent periods of practical experience and attended lectures at the institute for the insane in Kateřinská Street and other institutions.

Already in 1688 the need for practical demonstrations led to the establishment of an 'anatomical theatre' at Karolinum, and over time an anatomical institute developed from this. This comprised a dissection room, a large lecture hall, collections of chemical preparations and instruments, as well as an apartment for the profes-

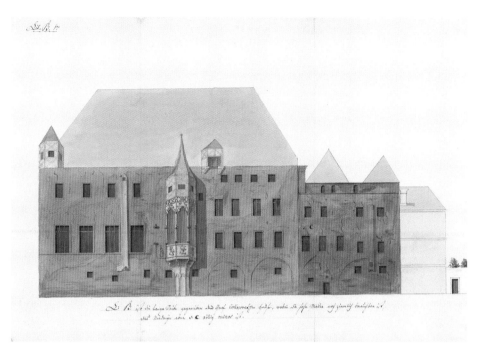

Southern façade of Karolinum with oriel before the Baroque reconstruction. Coloured draw-ing by architect František Maxmilián Kaňka from 1711. In his proposal for the reconstruction Kaňka recommended joining the two buildings and unifying the façade.

Western façade of Karolinum before the Baroque reconstruction. Coloured drawing by František Maxmilián Kaňka from 1711. In his proposal for reconstruction Kaňka recommend-ed removing the towers, unifying the façade and rebuilding the entry from Železná Street in the Baroque style.

sor of anatomy. In addition to the anatomical institute, Karolinum also contained a laboratory of medical chemistry, which also comprised a lecture hall, collections and an apartment for the professor. By the mid-19th century the Karolinum complex could no longer meet the needs of the modern institutes of the Medical Faculty (at the time anatomical, physiological, zoological, chemical and physical institutes) and Professor of Experimental Physiology Jan Evangelista Purkyně proposed constructing a building on Charles Square for the faculty. This project was not realized, but during the years 1857–1859 a new building was constructed in the neighbouring General Hospital in the New Town which provided premises for three institutes: pathology, forensic medicine and zoological-chemical. The medical institutes finally left Karolinum only at the end of the 1860s after the completion of the new buildings in the former Salma Garden opposite the General Hospital.

Competition between church representatives and the state for supervision over the university's life and study program dragged on for more than a century. A centralized state gradually gained the upper hand with regard to its own utilitarian needs, the developing economy and the industrialization of the Czech lands. State regulation came to the fore in particular in the period of high expenses for conducting wars. This process culminated in the Theresian and Josephine reforms in the second half of the 18th century. On the threshold of the industrial revolution and the formation of a civil society, the material demands on teaching also increased. Paradoxically it was the war-torn 17th century that brought support for the deeper study of the natural sciences and mathematics. Improvements in military technology in both offensive and defensive methods could not be devised without mathematics, land surveying and architectural knowledge in the construction of fortifications, as well as other technical disciplines, known as engineering.

At the time the title of *ingeniem* – that is, someone with skills and talent bordering on genius (from which the title of engineer is derived) – was given to the French marshal and engineer Sébastien le Prestre de Vauban, who in the service of Louis XIV built new types of forts and impregnable town fortifications, as well as siege weapons. One of his pupils was Christian Joseph Willenberg, the first professor to teach engineering studies in Prague. He taught in noble families, took part in the War of the Spanish Succession and decided to make use of his military-engineering knowledge by teaching selected pupils as a public teacher. In 1706 he sent a request, written in Czech, to this effect to Emperor Leopold I, who had Willenberg's capabilities examined by the military council at the imperial court. Willenberg successfully passed the exam, obtained the title of imperial engineer and on 18 January 1707 left Vienna for Prague, where he intended to practice. He was in possession of an imperial rescript which required the government of the Bohemia to ensure a regular salary for Willenberg so that he could teach pupils in military technology and the construction of fortifications. However, due to a lack of interest and insufficient funds this did not happen. Neither did the proposal of the mercantilists to establish a new department for Willenberg aimed at the teaching of geography and engineering sciences come to fruition. This proposal ran into opposition from leaders of the Jesuit College.

It was only after Willenberg made a new request, this time supported by Emperor Charles VI, who desperately needed capable young officers for leading victorious wars, that the Bohemian Estates government established a professorship financed from state funds on 9 November 1717. Willenberg began teaching in January 1718.

Rescript (first page) of Emperor Joseph I from 18 January 1707, addressed to the commissioners of the Land Diet of the Kingdom of Bohemia. In the rescript the emperor assents to the proposal of Christian Joseph Willenberg for the teaching of engineering and commands that Willenberg receive a regular salary for the teaching of 12 pupils. Even though this teaching only actually started 10 years later, the date of the rescript is regarded as the beginning of polytechnic education in Prague.

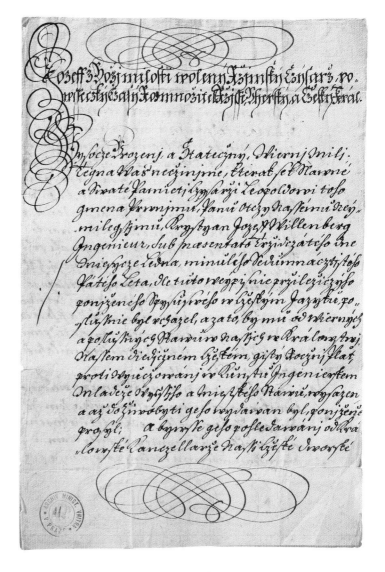

According to the project, his two-year course was supposed to provide theoretical and practical knowledge in the field of military engineering and the construction of fortifications so that graduates could immediately join the army engineering corps. At first teaching took place in Willenberg's apartment in the Saxon House in Mostecká Street in the Lesser Town, where the purchased books, models, instruments and other necessary items were also deposited. Even though Willenberg was able to teach as many as 12 students free of charge, at the beginning only nine applied, of whom several dropped out because of the demanding nature of the discipline. The teaching of military engineering itself only began after students had mastered advanced mathematics, such as trigonometry and logarithmic laws. Later he also taught mechanics, irrigation methods and the construction of weirs.

In 1726 Willenberg retired and was succeeded as professor of engineering by Johann Ferdinand Schor, who was then succeeded by František Herget. Herget excelled not only in his specialized technical knowledge, but also in the organizational talent with which he promoted improved technical knowledge in practical trades. He initiated regular lectures for Prague tradesmen and artisans on Sundays and holidays, at which he taught mainly mechanics. He also taught officials, primarily in the field of building, and provided instruction in engineering free of charge to Prague military cadets and officers. The number of students increased tenfold, the number of subjects offered also increased, and Herget needed assistance. For instance, he newly introduced the subject of drafting. His successful period in charge of the institute culminated in the acquisition of a decree on 17 April 1787, by which the hitherto Bohemian Estates department of engineering was incorporated in the Philosophy Faculty of Prague's university and Herget was appointed its professor. By the end of the 18th century the department at Klementinum already had – in addition to a professor – an assistant professor, two workshop masters, a machine hall, a lecture hall, a library and valuable collections in the fields of mathematical physics, geology and geography.

The further fate of the teaching of engineering sciences was influenced by František Josef Gerstner, university professor of mathematics and member of the imperial commission for the reform of general education. In accordance with the model of the École Polytechnique in Paris Gerstner recommended transforming engineering studies into a Bohemian Estates Polytechnic Institute. This recommendation was enacted into law by an imperial decree on 14 March 1803. In November 1806 Gerstner began teaching in the building of the former Jesuit seminary of Saint Wenceslas. He lectured in mathematics, but also in mechanics and hydraulics. He wrote a three-volume textbook of mechanics, in which he provided an exhaustive overview of the knowledge thus far attained in the subject. He was an outstanding personality with a broad view who worked on the threshold of the era of ironworks, railways and steam-powered engines. Students of the polytechnic spread his teachings into all kinds of fields. Gerstner was involved in the reconstruction and testing of Josef Božek's steam car, the first in Europe. In a number of fields the polytechnic carried on the work of the former engineering school, but it added the teaching of chemistry and agriculture, and at a later date also mineralogy.

In 1815 the Polytechnic Institute was separated from Prague's university by an imperial decree and became an independent place of education. Hundreds of students passed through its lecture halls. In the 1840s the number of students reached 1,500. They came mostly from Bohemia, mostly from the countryside, and two thirds of them declared themselves to be of Czech nationality. There were several polytechnic institutes in the Austrian monarchy at the time, but the Prague Polytechnic maintained its place as second, after the Vienna Polytechnic, in terms of its significance and the volume of teaching. Important physicist Christian Doppler worked at the polytechnic for 12 years, the famous Bernard Bolzano taught mathematics, and Josef Lumbe, who was the polytechnic's director in the years 1848 to 1863, improved the teaching of agriculture.

The students of Prague's university, along with those of the Jesuit Academy (later part of Charles-Ferdinand University) and those of the polytechnic, continued to contribute to the life of Prague. They lived in their own subculture, but also participated in public and political life. This particularly applied to times of crisis, social unrest and war, when Prague's towns found themselves under siege and students in the role of their defenders. The life of students in Prague in the early modern period underwent a number of changes, as the life of the city changed. Students continued to constitute an exceptional layer of society, endowed with many privileges. Nevertheless, most of them battled with poverty. They could try to improve their situation by singing carols, begging or the home teaching of younger pupils from rich families. They had to attend a stipulated number of lectures and disputa-

ANTONÍN LANGWEIL: **Klementinum – segment of model**, 1826–1837, paper. Prague City Museum.

ANTONÍN LANGWEIL: **Karolinum – segment of model**, 1826–1837, paper. Prague City Museum.

Antonín Langweil produced a model of Prague's historical centre from wood and paper in the years 1826–1837, inspired by a plaster model of Prague. He thus provided detailed evidence of the form of more than 2,000 buildings in Prague.

tions and take exams. Even though those students who came from Prague, which was a majority of them, did not have to pay for board and lodging, they still had the duty to pay fees for the awarding of university titles and exam certificates. Only the Jesuits at Klementinum College provided education free of charge up until 1618, undoubtedly in an attempt to attract students away from the university. Wax tablets and parchments were replaced by printed textbooks, while Scholasticism was replaced by humanist rhetoric. Travelling abroad for education became less common; only aristocratic young men visited foreign universities in the course of cavalier trips around Europe. However, the private lives of students were similar at all times. Teaching was not limited merely to developing the soul, but also the body. Teachers of fencing were active at the university and thus every student was supposed to be proficient with a rapier. This was part of the education of a cavalier with a view to current or future social standing. The teaching of dance also belonged to the age category of students, as did sporting tournaments in ballgames, riding competitions and the playing of bowls.

Academic freedoms continued to provide protection in the case of occasional outbreaks of indiscipline or conflicts with the protectors of public order. The university dealt with offences and transgressions with fines, corporal punishments (for instance, the humiliating and painful straddling of the wooden horse) and imprisonment either in the university's prison (carcer) or harsh imprisonment underground. It handed out various punishments for unauthorised duels, night-time rowdiness, theft, the seduction of young women with the promise of marriage, moving around the town without the mandatory lighting and other matters. The professors, including the Jesuits, generally had more understanding for youthful indiscretions than did the orderly town burghers. However, the university did not hand out punishments for serious crimes. In the case of murder, manslaughter, rape or insulting the head of state the university expelled the guilty party from its community and handed him over to the city courts for punishment.

Festivities, in particular those connected with university life, were an important part of student life. Humanism polished the rough and uncouth medieval student customs and gave them more dignity. The wild 'beánie' ritual, which had earlier accompanied the initiation of new students, took on the form of an orderly matriculation ceremony. The spontaneous festivals of fools and horse rides on the feast of Saint Nicolas were replaced by performances of student theatre with a fixed scenario and direction. Theatrical performances at Karolinum had taken place before the arrival of the Jesuits in Prague. However, the Jesuits at Klementinum developed the dramatic arts to a level of excellence previously unknown. Theatre served as a means for the teaching of languages and oratory, but also the teaching of faith. It also served the purpose of promoting the Jesuit order among the public. Even though the viewers could hardly understand the declaimed Latin texts, the impressive sets, costumes, musical accompaniment and the performances by the actors were sufficiently comprehensible for all those watching. Among the Jesuits there were a number of theoreticians of theatre and also actual dramatists. Students also took part in an opera by Jan Dismas Zelenka extolling the tradition of Saint Wenceslas. This opera was performed at the coronation ceremony in Prague of Charles VI and his wife in 1723. The university always had a significant role to play in coronation ceremonies. Public performances of music, song and ballet accompanied Christmas

Graduation ceremony in Karolinum's Aula Magna, as depicted by Prague engraver Augustin Neuräutter in 1711. At that time the head of the Aula faced in the direction of Železná Street.

and Easter festivities, as well as other important days in the liturgical calendar and the feast days of patron saints and the Virgin Mary. In the post-White Mountain era students established a special tradition of holding boat festivals on the Vltava (Moldau) river. On important occasions lanterns, accompanied by boats lighted with torches and carrying musicians and allegorical figures, were floated down the Vltava providing pleasure both to their makers and viewers. After the canonization of John of Nepomuk the boat festival became a regular part of the Navalis festivities held annually on May 15 in the saint's honour. The Jesuit student theatre had an excellent level and made a permanent contribution to Czech theatrical culture.

The university's supreme festivity was the graduation ceremony of doctors, even though not all students reached this stage because of the substantial expense involved. Other important festivities were the annual festival at the beginning of the school year, the installation of new rectors and the appointment of new deans. A central point of every festival was the procession and mass at the Tyn Church (Church of Our Lady before Tyn), which acted as the university's assembly place. Students were obliged to participate in all the opulent public church ceremonies during the year. The Jesuits skilfully incorporated student performances – whether musical, theatrical or declamatory – into the liturgical ceremonies. The burghers of Prague were entertained by the colourful spectacles and such promotion of the university in the public sphere helped it continue to attract donors from among the nobility.

One more bond between the students and the city of Prague must be mentioned: their role in the city's defence. The students owned weapons, were trained in their use and in times of threat they took up with youthful courage the role of the city's defenders, as a kind of home defence force. Already in 1639 they had helped defend Prague against the Swedes. They did so again in 1648, when they repelled the enemy on the ramparts and primarily defended Charles Bridge, thus preventing Swedish units from crossing from the left bank of the Vltava river to enter the Old Town on the right bank. The student legions distinguished themselves so well that they received their own battle standard and an armoury at Karolinum. Students from the Karolinum and Klementinum colleges fought in unison and gained recognition both from the Habsburg ruler, on whose behalf they defended Prague, and also from the Swedish enemy. The academic legion took part in the defence of Prague once again during the siege of 1741 and then again on two occasions during the Napoleonic wars. In each of these clashes they defended Prague, but at the same time the interests of the country's sovereign ruler – that is, the Habsburg dynasty.

Prague University started making preparations for the 500th anniversary of its foundation in 1848 five years in advance and magnificent celebrations were planned. A ten-member preparatory committee invited all universities in the Austrian monarchy and also those abroad, but primarily those universities in whose foundation Prague University had played some kind of role and which it therefore regarded as its 'daughters'. The celebrations of the university's anniversary included a ceremonial assembly for the award of honorary doctorates, the preparation of publications marking the jubilee and exhibitions to commemorate personalities from the university's past. Other parts of Charles-Ferdinand University's planned celebrations were the unveiling of a statue of its founder at the foot of Charles Bridge, the publication of a history of the university by Václav Vladivoj Tomek and the reconstruction of the dilapidated Karolinum.

Obrana staroměstké mostnj wěje. Vertheidigung des altstädter Brückenthurms.

Herausgegeben durch L. Bohmann's Erben.

Students from Karolinum and Klementinum associated in the academic legion defend the tower of Charles Bridge on the Old Town side against Swedish divisions of General Königsmark. They were led by Jan Kauffer, later a professor at the Law Faculty, and Jesuit Jiří Plachý. For their bravery in the defence of Prague (1648) the students received not only recognition, but also the right to use their own battle standard and a university arsenal. The painting by František Kolář from the first half of the 19th century idealizes their clothing, but not their enthusiasm.

The lists of domestic and foreign persons who were to be awarded honorary doctorates and honorary membership in the doctors' colleges of individual faculties were prepared with great care, because not only these persons were to be honoured, but also the university itself: the university's prestige would rise in accordance with the number of renowned and honourable people who were welcomed to Prague to receive honorary degrees. The selection of candidates was accompanied by long discussions and clashes of opinion. At that time there was a clash in the whole of Bohemian society between old Estates patriotism and new national revivalist tendencies. At the university itself adherents of various types of university reforms, such as the French and Humboldt models, put forward their respective arguments. In addition to this, in Prague a burgeoning Czech nationalism clashed with German

Der Eingang in das Karolinum zu Prag im März 1848. / Wchod do kolleje Karlowy w Praze w měsíci březnu 1848.

Verlag von Friedrich Kretzschmar in Prag.

Students at the entrance to Karolinum from Železná Street, pictured around their leader, author Uffo Horn, who on 15 March 1848 appealed to his colleagues to establish an armed student legion.

nationalism. In the end the selection of candidates for the awarding of honorary doctorates even reflected Pan-Slavism – the effort by some Czechs and other Slavs during this period to search for support in the form of links with other nations in the Slavic language group.

As a result of the revolutionary events in Prague, Vienna and a number of other European cities the jubilee celebrations, originally planned for 7 April 1848, were postponed several times. On the eve of the anniversary students and some pedagogues gathered in the courtyard of the Karolinum and celebrated the anniversary in their own way. Fortified by ten barrels of beer, which were rolled up from Karolinum's cellars on the rector's orders, they ceremonially set fire to the symbols of the old world: top hat, braids and a bureaucratic collar. They also experienced the atmosphere of the European 'spring of nations' two days later, when they ceremonially paraded through Stromovka park in the uniforms of the Student Legion. Those chosen for honorary degrees received their diplomas the following year by post. It was not until 31 January 1851 that the bronze statue of Charles IV, which was originally supposed to look out from its high pedestal to oversee the university's anniversary celebrations – marred by the revolutionary events – was finally unveiled on Křižovnické náměstí (Square of Knights of the Cross with the Red Star).

The university's anniversary celebrations were abandoned, but Prague University embarked with gusto on the process of modernization. The first university to make a petition to the Habsburg ruler was Vienna University, but Prague University followed soon afterwards. While barricades were already being built in the streets of Vienna, on 15 March Prague students composed their own petition and also formed an armed student legion. Among the important speakers at the meeting Josef Václav Frič and Uffo Horn gained popularity. They found support from Rector Jeroným Zeidler and also from Dean Augustin Smetana among members of the academic senate. The petition of the Prague students to the imperial ruler represented the demands of students of both the university and the polytechnic: they demanded the integration of the polytechnic in the university, equal standing for religious faiths at universities, freedom of teaching and research, the equal standing of Czech and German languages, study periods at foreign universities, reform of the examination system, the teaching of sport and the freedom to found student associations. The promised new code of study was supposed to accept the petition's demands. However, in fact these demands were subsequently fulfilled to various degrees and at different times. The merger of the university with the polytechnic never happened, while student associations started to arise almost immediately: Slavia, Teutonia, Markomania, Slovanská lípa (Slav Linden Tree) and others.

Students played a significant role in the armed clashes in Prague during the revolutionary events of 1848. However, in comparison with the year 1648 the situation was reversed: they no longer defended the interests of the country's ruler, but engaged against him, using the slogans of the revolutionary social classes of the European 'spring of nations', and with arms in hand also pursued their own interests. The radicalization of the students made itself apparent primarily in the formation of an armed

Dobytí Karolina.   II.   Einnahme des Carolinum.

Windisch-Graetz's troops occupy Karolinum on 12 June 1848. Students also built barricades in front of the polytechnic and Klementinum, where the Student Legion had its main command. Lithograph by Bedřich Anděl to a design by Felix Roscher.

student legion on 16 March. The legion had as many as 3,600 men, of whom almost half were represented by a cohort of the Prague Polytechnic. The university's philosophical, juridical and medical faculties each contributed one cohort. Representatives of the legion dressed in a uniform, or at least wore clearly recognizable parts of this uniform. However, at the time they were not differentiated by nationality. The legion was led by the mayor of Prague himself and professors appointed by the university senate. Students themselves commanded only lower-level units – centuriums. Dissatisfaction and tension on the streets of Prague were only intensified by the threats of Alfred I, Prince of Windisch-Graetz (Windischgrätz), the military commander of the Bohemian Lands. The unrest culminated in the building of barricades and an armed uprising on the part of the inhabitants of Prague with a substantial participation by students. The emperor's troops conquered Karolinum and Klementinum by force. While the townspeople and the National Guard lost their courage and abandoned the barricades, the students remained at arms. On 17 June Prague capitulated and the students paid a heavy price for their opposition to the government army: some paid with their lives, while others paid with their health, exile or forced conscription into the army. In January 1849 the student legion was dissolved. Two renewed and active student clubs – that is, the Czech Academic Reading Club and the German Akademische Lese und Redehalle – prefigured the nationalist split of students for almost a further hundred years.

The mid-19th century saw a significant growth of interest in artistic and art-historical fields of study among the Prague intellectual elite. The beginnings of the artistic universities, which initially did not have the statutory form of universities, emerged from the spiritual needs and cultural life of the aristocracy, but were also connected with the development of industrialization in the second half of the 19th century. These factors were gradually supplemented by the need for the development of an intellectual culture for modern civil society – a process in which Prague played a significant role in view of its long tradition.

The Academy of Fine Arts as the first place of artistic higher education in Prague was promoted by a small group of leading Bohemian aristocrats, members of the Society of Patriotic Friends of the Arts. This was founded in 1796 as the first Bohemian charitable association for the support of the fine arts at the initiative of Count Franz Joseph Sternberg-Manderscheid and painter Jan Jakub Quirin Jahn. The society was founded on the model of similar charitable societies, for instance in Nuremberg and Leipzig. However, the situation in Prague was somewhat specific – more pressing. Art objects from the monasteries and churches abolished by the Josephine reforms were easy booty for traders, while artistic treasures from Prague Castle were removed to Vienna. Members of the society joined forces *to try to halt the decline in artistic taste, limit the export from the homeland of those works of art that still remain in Prague and support the foundation of an art gallery and an academy of arts*.

The art gallery was founded in the same year, while the academy of arts began teaching four years later. It was only on 10 September 1799 that Emperor Francis I issued an imperial decree allowing the society to found the academy and allocating it space in the Klementinum complex. The academy's first director and for the first two years its only teacher was the painter Josef Bergler. There was strong interest in studying at the academy operated by the Society of Patriotic Friends of the Arts, even though at the beginning the academy taught only drawing. In the third year of its operation the academy already had 17 students. Courses in graphic design and landscape painting were gradually added. Josef Mánes was among the graduates of the course in landscape painting. The academy gained fame in particular after 1841, when Kristián Ruben became its director. Ruben, who had been educated at the academies in Düsseldorf and Munich, established new ateliers for the teaching of sculpture and architecture. There was an increased interest in studying at the academy and in 1846 a total of 186 students were registered there.

After Ruben left for the academy in Vienna in 1852, none of his successors succeeded in adapting the academy to new artistic trends. Talented individuals left to study abroad, primarily to Paris. In the longer perspective the significance of the Prague academy fell for three decades. Under the influence of aristocratic sponsors a cold academic approach continued to prevail and the academy failed to reflect the social ferment of an emerging civic society. The academy only experienced an upturn again with the onset of the generation of the Czech National Theatre (opened in 1881) and the return of artists from study abroad. In the 1880s the teaching of theoretical subjects, including the history of art, was also improved. After the foundation of the Academy of Arts, Architecture & Design in Prague (AAAD – later

KAREL VÍTĚZSLAV MAŠEK: **Poster of the Exhibition of Architecture and Engineering**, 1898, coloured lithography.

A representative of symbolism and Art Nouveau, Mašek studied at the Prague Academy of Fine Arts and later became professor of decorative painting at the Academy of Arts, Architecture & Design in Prague.

known as UMPRUM) in 1885, which had the clear aim of propagating taste and art in industrial production using wood, stone, glass, textiles and other materials, the Academy of Fine Arts gained a strong competitor, and thus also new motivation. Both academies gained from the mutual competition; there were links between them and some important artistic figures worked as pedagogues at both institutions. For a certain period the two artistic schools shared the same premises in a new building built in 1882 at Rejdiště, now named Jan Palach Square (Náměstí Jana Palacha).

In 1896 the legal status of the Academy of Fine Arts underwent a fundamental change, when its ownership was transferred to the state. The change was initiated by a group of new sponsors, headed by successful Czech entrepreneurs Josef Hlávka and Vojtěch Lanna. Together with Karel Buquoy, they achieved their aim after several years of efforts at reform. The academy was one of only three of its kind in the Austrian monarchy (alongside those in Vienna and Krakow) and provided education in the fields of painting and sculpture. It was one of the leading institutions of its type in Europe. Julius Mařák, who was appointed rector for the academic year 1887/88, prepared new statutes for the academy, which fundamentally changed its orientation. He attempted to replace the academy's academic and historically based approach with one that emphasized personal creative effort on the part of students. The newly established department of sculpture at the academy was headed from 1896 by Josef Václav Myslbek. In 1891 the academy acquired studios in one of the pavilions that remained after the jubilee exhibition at the Výstaviště exhibition halls in Stromovka park and later, in the years 1897–1903, a new building in Letná district. The period of study was five or six years, except for sculpture, which at the beginning was three years. Teaching took place in ateliers of individual professors.

The imperial Academy of Arts, Architecture & Design in Prague was legally established by a statute issued by the Ministry of Culture and Education on 15 October 1885. The academy was founded *with the aim of providing education to equip students with the skills for using the arts in industry and also of educating teachers in the field of industrial arts*. A similar academy of applied arts had already been founded in Vienna much earlier, in 1867, and at the beginning this served as a model for the new academy in Prague. The foundation of the Academy of Arts, Architecture & Design in Prague fitted in well with the monarchy's attempt to create a network of specialized universities as a basis for the state's economic development. However, the immediate motivation was an attempt at emancipation on the part of the Czech-speaking intelligentsia, which precisely in the 1880s culminated in the division of Charles-Ferdinand University into separate Czech and German universities, the opening of the National Theatre, the building of the National Museum and other activities. The academy's program of study was based on a new conception of the relationship between production and art, respectively on the need to find a balance between rapid industrialization and the aesthetic level of industrial products. A romanticism that extolled the beauty of traditional hand-crafted trades led to attempts to promote graceful and noble forms also in the case of industrial production.

The term 'artistic industry' was introduced by German architect Gottfried Semper in 1852 in his book Science, Industry and Art (*Wissenschaft, Industrie und Kunst*). All over Europe specialized schools were being founded for the teaching of good taste and for the promotion of noble aesthetics in the production of objects of a decorative nature. The first director of the imperial Academy of Arts, Architecture & Design in

Prague was architect Josef Schmoranz. Teaching started in 1885 in both Czech and German, and students paid tuition fees. The courses were not open to women. A ladies academy for artistic embroidery and a school for jewellery and decoration were opened, and there were also evening courses in drawing for women. The teaching of drawing and modelling was supplemented by theoretical lectures on the history of art, taught by Otakar Hostinský and Karel B. Mádl, and other related subjects (descriptive geometry, anatomy, chemistry of colours and others). The academy gradually developed and the number of specialisms at higher levels increased. Well-known figures joined as pedagogues, as new subjects were added to the curriculum.

The Academy of Arts, Architecture & Design was somewhat harmed by the transformation of the Academy of Fine Arts into a state educational institution. However, thanks to Jan Kotěra it gained a new direction of study. The industrial arts academy became a significant centre of the Art Nouveau movement and it acquired orders for producing artistic proposals for a wide range of objects, ranging from furniture to ceramics, glass, jewellery, textiles, embroidery and other materials. The work of the academy's pedagogues and also of its students was successfully presented at international and domestic exhibitions. Jan Kotěra was replaced as head of the academy in 1910 by Slovene architect Josip Plečnik, under whose leadership several students who later went on to become excellent architects completed their studies at the academy. There were repeated negotiations aimed at raising the academy to the level of a university of decorative arts or an academy of applied arts, but the academy did not achieve university status until 1946 under a new name, the University of Decorative Arts (UMPRUM).

In the middle of the 19th century the state norms determining the statutory form of university education, which were based on a traditional – in some ways still medieval – conception of education, were replaced by new norms bringing them into line with modern notions of the capitalist era. The first herald of changes to come at the Prague university were the attempts to give the Czech language equal status to that of the German language in teaching, even though in some specializations the Czech language did not yet possess the necessary technical terminology and these subjects continued to be taught in German. German had a head start from the year 1784, when it replaced Latin as the language of instruction in most subjects. The law on the reorganization of universities issued on 30 September 1849 bears the name of its proposer, Minister of Culture and Education Leopold, count of Thun and Hohenstein. Professorial bodies were newly placed at the head of faculties. These bodies elected a dean for a one-year term of office and took decisions on the appointment of new professors from the ranks of staff who had completed their post-doctoral qualifications (habilitation). This system lasted for the entire century.

At a time of increasing state influence on the organization of universities, it was not only the system of teaching that underwent changes, but also the social life of teachers and students. Even though the freedom to found societies and professional associations was only formally legalized by the law of assembly from 1867, a certain political thawing came about already at the turn of the 1850s and 1860s and there was a growth in student associations – thus far informal – which held lectures, public readings, debates on expert subjects, but also excursions and dances. The Czech fraternities included primarily the Academic Reading Club and later specialized clubs differentiated by profession or by region, such as the Všehrd legal club,

Reminders of the rich life of student associations before the First World War: Almanac of Czech student body, published by the Academic Reading Association in Prague in 1869 on its 20th anniversary – Ex libris label from the library of the Všehrd association of Czech lawyers with its symbol – Standard of Czech students, given as a gift to French student representatives at the 2nd international students congress in Paris in 1900 – Standard of the Lese- und Rede-halle der deutschen Studenten in Prag (Reading Hall of German Students in Prague) from the second half of the 19th century – Student May celebrations at Prague Exhibition Grounds in the year 1899 – Order-of-dance card at ball of Czech medical students in 1914.

the Association of Czech Medical Doctors, the Historical Club, the Association of Czech Chemists and the Union of Czech Mathematicians and Physicists. Czech regional clubs included central Bohemian club Jungmann, Plzeň-region Radbuza, south Bohemian Štítný and east Bohemian Krakonoš. German students founded similar associations (Burschenschaft) and Jewish students also founded their own clubs. In a period when the highlight of the social season was the ball, the student associations of jurists, philosophers, medical students and technical students all competed with each other to hold the most lavish ball. Most active in competing for social prestige in holding ballroom dances were law and medical students. Members of the ball committees planned well in advance. They contacted influential members of society and invited them to attend their ball or at least to make a sponsorship contribution. The funds thus acquired were used to cover the costs of putting on the ball (at the medical doctors' ball in January 1864 at Žofín Palace there were three firework shows), but especially for the support of poor students.

The 1864 medical ball, at which the order-of-dance cards were printed in both Czech and German, was perhaps one of the last conciliatory gestures of the student movement, which shortly afterwards split along national lines, as did academic clubs. Czech students frequented different pubs, coffee houses, literary salons, theatre productions and churches than their German colleagues did. In Prague itself they even sought accommodation in different quarters of the city: Czech students preferred the streets in the vicinity of Charles (Karlovo) Square and Wenceslas Square in the New Town, while German students usually lived in the Old Town or in the vicinity of Příkopy and Hybernská streets in the New Town. German students held their weekly corso (social promenade) along Příkopy Street, while Czech students held theirs along National Boulevard (Národní třída), and woe betide anyone who turned up there in white knee-high socks or in the uniform of one of the German Burschenschaft student fraternities. Over time competition between the two nationalities degenerated into expressions of mutual hatred. Perhaps the most infamous 'battle' between members of Czech and German student clubs took place on an excursion to the village of Chuchle near Prague in 1881.

The nationalist and later also racial feelings amongst students, notably the language division, merely reflected the atmosphere in the whole of society, in particular among the intellectual elites. It is noteworthy that a complete rift between the two nations in the Bohemian Lands did not occur first at the famous old Charles-Ferdinand University, but rather at the relatively young technical university, the polytechnic. Already during the revolutionary year of 1848 the polytechnic's students were in the front ranks of the revolutionaries. They had substantially the largest representation in the academic legion: almost half of all men in this legion belonged to the polytechnic's cohort, which had a Czech leadership. The defeat of the revolution resulted in repression against student leaders: some of them ended up in jail, while others were forcibly conscripted into the Austrian army. However, this had hardly any effect on interest in study at the polytechnic. Demand did not decline even after another polytechnic institute started teaching in Brno in 1850. The new Brno polytechnic was rather frequented by students from Moravia, from where students had previously gone to Vienna.

In the 1850s the Prague polytechnic struggled with major problems of lack of teaching space and a poor level of prior preparation on the part of students. Graduates of the lower and higher technical schools (Realschule or reálka – schools which specialized in mathematics and natural science), of which there were more than 20 in Bohemia by 1860, arrived at the polytechnic relatively well prepared. However, the classical grammar schools did not provide sufficient preparation for study at a polytechnic. From the academic year 1864/65 a school-leaving exam certificate was a condition for acceptance at the polytechnic. The polytechnic found a temporary solution to its lack of space by leasing the Liechtenstein Palace in the Kampa district, at which lectures in civil engineering and chemistry were held. The prestige of polytechnic institutes around Europe rose proportionately to the development of technical sciences and the pressing need for specialists for growing industry. At the beginning of the 1860s three important professors – Rudolf Skuherský (who lectured in Czech from 1861), K. Jelínek and Karel Kořistka – were responsible for the reorganization of the Prague polytechnic on the model of the most modern European technical universities. The result of their efforts was the Organic Statute of the Polytechnic Institute, approved by the ruler on 23 November 1863. This legislative act transformed the Prague polytechnic into a real university. The hitherto powers of appointed directors were taken over by an annually elected rector, teaching in Czech and German were granted equal status and the number of professors was doubled. The four main fields of study were prototypes for the future faculties: water and road engineering, civil engineering, mechanical engineering and chemistry. The statute also prescribed compulsory lectures and stipulated an organizational order.

Rivalry between Czech and German professors soon became a sensitive issue and resulted six years later on 8 April 1869 in the division of Prague's polytechnic into a Czech Polytechnic Institute and a German Polytechnic Institute. Professors were given the choice of which institute they wished to teach at and the library remained joint property. In 1874 the Czech Polytechnic Institute moved to a new building on Charles Square, built to a plan by Vojtěch Ignác Ullmann, and in 1875 both institutes, which until that time had been under the Land Estates government, were taken into state ownership. Any graduate who passed two prescribed state exams continued to have the right to use the title engineer. The polytechnic did not gain the right to award doctorate degrees in technical sciences until the passing of an imperial law in 1901. Interest in obtaining a doctorate was strongest among students of chemistry. One year later the lecture halls were opened for the first time to female students. On the threshold of the First World War the polytechnic had around 3,000 students and a firm place in civic society. With the awakening of Prague political life in the 1870s and 1880s expressions of professional solidarity among both students and graduates of technical disciplines also intensified. This was reflected in specialized journals, clubs and associations, some of which continue to this day – for instance, the Association of Czech Chemists, founded in 1872.

From the 1860s onward, together with the increase in educational level among Czech speakers, the Czech language was used more and more widely at the universities. For instance, at the Philosophy Faculty, at which disciplines from both the humanities and natural sciences were taught, the relative proportion between the two nations of Bohemia changed in a short time. While in the 1860s 54% of those graduating with doctorates considered themselves of Czech nationality, in the 1870s this figure had risen to 69%. The growing potential of the Czech intellectual community is also made evident, for instance, by the 11-volume encyclopaedia known as Rieger's Encyclopaedia. The encyclopaedia, published over a period of 15 years, attested not only specialist erudition, but also a rich Czech terminology in a number of fields. Thus an argument against giving Czech equal status to German at the university – that Czech lacked specialist terminology – ceased to be valid. This argument had been used by German liberals in the Viennese government repeatedly since 1848, even though in the 1860s teaching was already conducted in the local national languages at the universities in Budapest, Krakow and Lviv (Lvov). Among the strongest opponents of granting equal status to the Czech language were some important lawyers at the Prague university – even as late as the 1860s, when Czech students were in the majority at the Law Faculty and discussions were already taking place on the division of the university into separate Czech and German entities. Nationalism had a detrimental effect on university life. It held back teaching and research, but on the other hand it encouraged competition.

After complicated discussions and disputes, the political negotiations resulted in an imperial decree of 11 April 1881 which divided Charles-Ferdinand University into two universities: one with German as the language of instruction and the other with

The Hlávka student college, built in the years 1903–1904 according to plans by Josef Fanta. Jenštejnská 1966/1, Prague 2.

Czech. Both continued to be called Charles-Ferdinand and both rectorates were located at Karolinum. The Czech university began teaching in the 1882/83 academic year, initially only at the philosophy and law faculties, and at the medical faculty one year later. In order to ensure an equal standard and continuity of teaching, and to compete effectively with the German university, the Czech university needed to find additional teaching staff. Already since the 1870s it had been looking around for appropriate personalities at other universities, as well as encouraging promising junior staff at the university to pass their post-doctoral exam (habilitation). Tomáš G. Masaryk, hitherto a lecturer at the university in Vienna, was recruited as a new professor at the Philosophy Faculty of the new Czech university. There was substantially greater fluctuation at the German university: some pedagogues arrived from Vienna, Berlin and German regional universities to teach in Prague, while others left Prague for these universities. Albert Einstein also spent a period in Prague in the 1911/12 academic year.

In addition to dealing with personnel problems, both universities also had to struggle with serious problems of lack of space, in particular in the fields of medicine and the natural sciences, which were developing quickly in the content and extent of their teaching. Joseph II's reforms in the second half of the 18th century had already changed the health system and strengthened state supervision by the use of so-called regional physicians. At the end of the 18th century a state order of the centralized absolutist state led to the first female students entering the grounds of the university (students of midwifery courses), though lecture halls were not opened up to regular female students until the end of the 19th century.

The practical teaching of medicine was carried out, as before, in cooperation with hospitals and charitable institutions, primarily Prague hospitals. The university did not have sufficient funds to establish its own clinics, but it had to ensure appropriate premises and equipment for theoretical instruction. Already at the end of the middle of the 19th century the lecture halls at Karolinum were no longer fit for purpose and the Medical Faculty left them in the 1860s. The first institutes for medical studies were established in the neighbouring General Hospital. During the course of the second half of the 19th century these were supplemented by land plots in the southern part of the New Town in the vicinity of Ke Karlovu and Na Slupi streets, where the significant university complex known today as Albertov was established. Albertov street itself, roughly half a kilometre long, was named in 1905 after Czech surgeon Dr. Eduard Albert, who found fame as a professor of medicine at Vienna University after he was rejected by the university in Prague. Medical fields such as anatomy, pathology, physiology and forensic medicine – and later also specialisms in the natural sciences, mathematics and physics – found dignified premises in the Albertov complex, which was continually expanded even during the period of the First Czechoslovak Republic. The Albertov complex, whose buildings were used by both the Czech and German universities, represented a new modern phenomenon in urban architecture and also in society.

Already before the First World War the rapid development of university education and teaching led to another problem in Prague – student accommodation. Some students lived at home with their parents, some continued to live in 'digs' – shared rented accommodation – while others commuted to Prague. Students at technical polytechnics were particularly hard hit by the lack of accessible accommodation: in comparison with university students, a much higher percentage of these students came from the countryside. The medieval conception of colleges as a common household – the workshops of a master and his pupils – had long ago changed its sense and content. In the modern period colleges became accommodation facilities for students, which fulfilled the practical needs of students to a varying extent. At the initiative of successful entrepreneur and builder Josef Hlávka, and with his financial support, the Association of Student Colleges of Czech Universities in Prague established a model college, called Hlávka College (also known as Hlávka Colleges, as there are two buildings), in Jenštejnská Street in the New Town. Opened in November 1904, the college was built over a period of two years and was intended to serve the needs of poor students with exceptional academic results – primarily Czech students of technical disciplines. The project undoubtedly reflected Hlávka's own experiences of hardship from the time of his studies. The simply equipped two-bed rooms provided accommodation for 215 students and had electric lighting and central heating. Paid staff took care of food and washing. The two basic conditions of acceptance to the college were poverty and excellent academic performance, but sponsor Hlávka added further conditions: those accommodated were obliged to attend a course in one of the major world languages and also to train in fencing in order to maintain a good physical condition.

Sporting Activities of Prague Students

Athletic and gymnastics section of University Sports Association 1912 – Doc. František Smotlacha with light athletes of Prague University Sports Association, 1926 – Light athletics meeting between students of Charles University and the Czech Technical University in 1930s – Charles University's basketball team in 1930s – Ice-hockey team of Prague University Sports Association at III International Academic Sports Championships, Bardonecchia in Italy 1933 – University students performing exercises at the Marathon Gymnastics Institute, 1936

At the time of the closure of Czech universities in 1939 there were 10 student colleges in operation in Prague, partly or wholly financed from the funds of various foundations and associations, which accommodated a total of more than 3,500 students. Decisive for obtaining a place at one of them was not so much the type of university or the subject studied, but rather students were selected according to their political sympathies and membership of an association. Common accommodation at colleges introduced new elements of collectivism, solidarity and organization into student life. The common life of students received a new impulse when the first female students entered the lecture halls. However, not all faculties were willing to open their doors at once. While the first female students graduated from the philosophy and medical faculties, as well as in technical disciplines, at the very threshold of the 20th century, they were only allowed to sign up to study at the Law Faculty in 1918.

Both Charles-Ferdinand universities in Prague, the Czech one and the German one, as well as both polytechnics, were substantially involved in Prague's political life. Members of the academic corps engaged in specialist societies and in political parties. In the tense nationalist political atmosphere before First World War an influential part of the academic body of the German university attempted to gain support in Berlin. For this purpose the German Charles Ferdinand University awarded a honorary degree to German Emperor Wilhelm II – in the field of medicine. Absolutely unprecedented political nonsense. Even though the Czech and German universities did not communicate with each other very much, at the beginning of the 1914–1918 Great War they agreed on loyalty to the Habsburg throne. Evidence of this stance is provided by public speeches, participation in celebrations of the monarch's anniversary and demonstrative gestures of support for the 'victorious weapons' of Austria-Hungary. However, pedagogues at the Czech University were not united in their stance toward the state. Some of them continued to defend the historical rights of the Kingdom of Bohemia, while others openly refused to support the military efforts of the monarchy. A significant event was the decision of both universities, Czech and German, to award in unison on 29 January 1917 an honorary doctor of law degree to newly acceded Habsburg monarch Charles I. Some Czech professors, some of whom had participated directly in the successor's education and knew him personally, hoped that he would soon end the war, which he had not started, and that he would be well-disposed toward the demands of the nations living in the empire. An opposing program advocating an independent democratic national state was promoted by Professor Tomáš Garrigue Masaryk, who was living abroad, and his adherents at the Czech Charles-Ferdinand University.

It was a considerably weakened academic community of the Prague universities that welcomed the declaration of an independent Czechoslovak Republic by the National Committee on 28 October: both students and teachers had served in the trenches at the fronts during the war that had just ended. The one-time adherents of a democratic autonomous arrangement within the empire soon accepted the achieved solution, confirmed by the victorious powers, whose leading representatives were in turn awarded honorary doctorates by Prague University, just as T. G. Masaryk had been. The inter-war republic maintained the substantial statutory changes to the university system introduced in the mid-19th century by the Thun-Hohenstein reforms. State power in the form of party bureaucracy had an ever greater say in the modern Czechoslovak education system. This is evident in the extension of the network of Czech universities, the number of which grew to 15 during the inter-war period, as it was the state that made the decision on the foundation of these new universities. Charles University in Prague, which reverted to this name following a change to the law in 1920, maintained a dominant position. The hitherto Deutsche Karls-Ferdinand Universität was renamed the Deutsche Universität in Prag (German University in Prague), and in the new circumstances the possibility of relocating it to Liberec, which was a traditional centre of scientific research in the German-speaking regions, was even considered. Charles University was the only one to retain the statutory features of a corporative organization, even if only after two years of dispute. It was only a verdict of the Supreme Administrative Court in October 1922 that finally removed all police supervision over Charles University. The state retained a number of decision-making and supervisory powers: for instance, the approval and payment of state senior lecturers, as well as of regular and exceptional professors, who in the end were more or less formally appointed by the president of the republic.

A decree of the Ministry of Education and National Enlightenment of the Czechoslovak Republic from 1 September 1920 also substantially changed Prague's second largest university. The polytechnic was given a new name and a new legal status. Under the name Czech Technical University in Prague (CTU) it comprised a group of seven universities: the University of Civil Engineering, the University of Architecture and Building Construction, the University of Mechanical and Electrical Engineering, the University of Chemical Technology, the University of Agriculture and Forestry, the University of Special Studies and the University of Business (which was incorporated in the CTU in 1929 and had the greatest number of students). The former German Technical University was renamed Deutsche Technische Hochschule in Prag and, like the Deutsche Universität in Prag, continued to operate without interruption until the end of the Second World War.

In contrast, all Czech universities were closed by a decision of the Nazi-run Protectorate administration on 17 November 1939. Subsequently, in 1945 on the symbolic date of 17 November, both German universities in Prague were abolished as part of the university network of the German Third Reich. Teaching at the Academy of Fine Arts was also interrupted during the years 1939–1945, but the closure did not apply to the School of Decorative Arts, as this did not achieve university status until 1946.

Disputes concerning the extent of academic freedoms of universities in relation to the state and the legal form of these freedoms continued throughout the entire 20th century. Universities lost their academic freedoms in a law passed in 1950. A law in 1966 partially restored these freedoms and a law in 1980 took them away once again.

The post-war enthusiasm with which pedagogues and students returned to the lecture halls in May 1945 was soon dampened by unfavourable political developments and the communist takeover in February 1948. The new university law of 1950 abolished the autonomy of universities and academic senates, which had been the bearer of this autonomy. It also abolished the awarding of titles and the designation of graduates by professional degrees. In accordance with the Soviet model, teaching and research was allowed to continue to exist only in direct subordination to Marxist-Leninist ideology and the organs of the Communist Party. New definitions and organization of departments enabled manipulation and control in this sense.

The system of Prague universities underwent changes. On the one hand, this was the result of a real need caused by the expanding number and increasing complexity of academic disciplines; on the other hand, of a strained attempt to interrupt the continuity of democratic science and to subject science and teaching to an ideological diktat reflecting the Marxist theory of communism as the highest level of development. A new artistic university, the Academy of Performing Arts (AMU), focused on film, theatre, music and dance, was founded in response to the real needs of modern society and the development of media technologies. On more than one occasion students and pedagogues of this university were at the head of the cultural avant-garde during the political changes of the second half of the 20th century.

Charles University gradually increased the number of its faculties. From 1953 onwards, the university had not one, but three medical faculties, and in the same year it established an independent Faculty of Mathematics and Physics. In 1965 a Faculty of Physical Education and Sport was established and in 1972 a Faculty of Journalism. In 1990 three theological faculties were incorporated into the university and a Faculty of Social Sciences was established, while the year 2000 saw the establishment of a Faculty of Humanities.

In 1952 the large departments of chemistry and of agriculture-forestry were removed from the Czech Technical University (CTU) and two new independent Prague universities were established: the University of Agriculture (from 1995 the Czech University of Agriculture in Prague – in 2007 its official English name was changed to the Czech University of Life Sciences in Prague) and the University of Chemistry and Technology in Prague.

The organization of the teaching of economic disciplines underwent a complicated development. Before the war the business school had been a part of CTU and its transformation into an independent university in the post-war period – as the University of Economic Sciences – was originally motivated by the specific needs of the discipline. However, already in 1948 planners of the ideological transformation of education had determined a new name and a new mission for this school. The University of Political and Economic Sciences (UPES), established in 1949 according to the Soviet model, was planned as an elite Marxist university. It was supposed to spread the new conceptions of science and politics into the wider university environment with the aim of establishing a new socialist intelligentsia as quickly as possible and thus replacing the so-called bourgeois intelligentsia. At the same time the demand for the rapid education of a working-class intelligentsia was also implemented, and so a number of students came directly from the factories or started university study after only a short period of preparation. However, the inconsistency of this conception led to its failure. In 1953 the UPES experiment was abolished. Neither did some other universities founded in Prague with a predominantly ideological motivation last long: for instance, the University of Russian Language and Literature (1953–1960) and the 17 November University (1961–1974), which was established for students from developing countries.

An indirect successor of the UPES is the University of Economics in Prague, which has been operating with standard academic faculties since September 1953 and today is the fourth largest university in Prague. The youngest higher education facility in Prague of a university type is the Police Academy, founded in 1993 and demonstrating the important role the state assigns to expertise in the field of security law.

At a time when Prague universities were trying to find their place in the new societal arrangements after the first and second world wars they also had to deal with problems inherited from the past, in particular the greater space required for scientific research by a growing number of specialized fields of study, such as astronomy, physics, chemistry, geography and others hitherto pursued at the Philosophy Faculty. This era resulted first of all in the removal in 1920 of the subjects of mathematics and natural science from the Philosophy Faculty and the foundation of independent natural science faculties. The establishment of these faculties had been prepared at the beginning of the 20th century, but the war delayed the construction of new buildings in the Albertov complex. The university's botanical garden, founded in 1898, was incorporated in the Natural Sciences Faculty. New buildings of specialized institutes were gradually added to the complex, and teaching as well as theoretical and applied research were transferred to these new buildings.

Both universities, the Czech entity and the German university, which in the period of the First Republic only had roughly half as many students as the Czech university, aimed to construct new central university buildings and modern faculties, concentrated as far as possible in one complex in one of the districts of Prague, for instance Podskalí or Letná hill. At the threshold of the 20th century the Prague civic authorities decided to redevelop extensive areas in the Josefov and Old Town districts for public health and urban planning reasons, and Czech and German universities received land plots at the foot of Čechův most (Čech Bridge) and opposite Rudolfinum. According to a plan, both rectorates, as well as both juridical and theological faculties, were to occupy new premises near Čechův most, while a land plot at today's Jan Palach Square was from the beginning intended for the Czech university's

Student record book of Jan Opletal, student at the Medical Faculty of Charles University, fatally shot in Prague on 28 October 1939, the anniversary of the foundation of the Czechoslovak Republic, during a demonstration against the German occupiers.

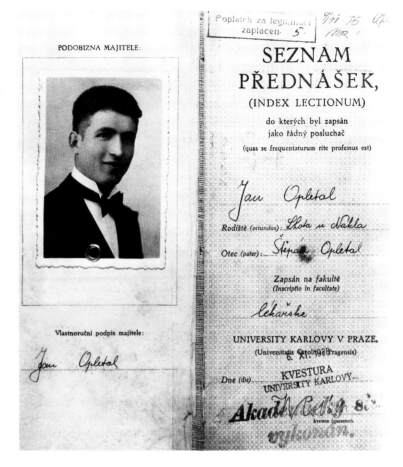

Prague, 15 November 1939. Thousand-strong protest march at the funeral of student Jan Opletal, the first student to become a victim of Nazi despotism.

Prague, 17th November 1939. Decree of the Reichsprotector Konstantin von Neurath on the closure of Czech universities for a period of three years. It also announces the execution of nine Czech university students and the internment of a 'large number' of them.

In 1939 around 1,200 Czech university students – not only from Prague, but also from Brno and Příbram – were transported for forced labour to the concentration camp at Sachsenhausen, where hunger, hard labour and in some cases death awaited them. Many of those who were not arrested left the republic illegally in order to join the exile army.

Prague, 1st September 1940, German university students march through Prague.

Philosophy Faculty. The design of the new buildings of the German university was entrusted to architect Josef Zasche, while the rector of the Czech university chose Professor Jan Kotěra for this task.

Several years of hard preparatory work on the part of the two architects and discussions about the projects for new central buildings for both universities were interrupted by the outbreak of the First World War. Neither was the grandiose project realized during the first years of the First Republic. In the end Charles University acquired the use of a number of buildings in the new university complex on the right bank of the Moldau (Vltava) river: a new building at Břehová Street 7, built in the years 1920–1922, the building of the Philosophy Faculty at Jan Palach Square, completed in 1930, and the Law Faculty, completed in 1931. The medical and natural science faculties found a home in the Albertov complex, and later at Motol and in Vinohrady respectively. Efforts to ensure appropriate premises for university faculties and to build colleges to provide sufficient accommodation space for students continued during the further decades of the 20th century and continue even today. One significant achievement of the period since the Second World War has been the gradual reconstruction of the rectorate at Karolinum into a dignified head office of Charles University and the reconstruction of the entire university complex between

The march by students to Prague Castle on 25 February 1948 in protest against the communist putsch and in support of President Eduard Beneš. Around 2,000 students took part in the silent march, which set out from the building of the Czech Technical University on Charles Square. Students were one of the few who feared the loss of democracy and who publicly demonstrated against the onset of totalitarianism. In Neruda Street the march was met by a unit of the State Security Service. The unit's violent intervention against the marchers led to injury and bloodshed.

Růžena Vacková, professor of classical archaeology at Charles University's Philosophy Faculty, took part in the protest march on 25 February 1948 together with her students. At the first sitting of the corps of professors after the march she raised a protest against the police intervention. Her subsequent fate was shared by dozens of other democratically oriented university pedagogues and students: a ban on lecturing, expulsion from the university, prosecution on charges of treason and espionage in a show-trial, many years of imprisonment, and in the case of three students of Charles University execution. Teachers such as Růžena Vacková and Jan Patočka, who had made an oath at their graduation to spread education and truth, were only able to fulfil this oath by prison lectures and later seminars held in private apartments.

Fruit Market (Ovocný trh) and Celetná and Kamzíková streets according to plans by Professor Jaroslav Fragner and his successors.

Since its foundation the Czech Technical University (CTU) had also struggled with a lack of space. In the first years following the establishment of Czechoslovakia the CTU's rectors joined forces with the leadership of Charles University in efforts to acquire new buildings and pushed for the implementation of an older plan to build a new university campus on Letná hill. However, in the end a more modest project was chosen: proposed by Antonín Engel, this was aimed at meeting the needs of all the universities associated within the framework of the CTU by constructing new buildings on free land plots in the Dejvice district. On 21 June 1925, the foundation stone was ceremonially laid in the presence of the president of the republic and the prime minister. However, the ambitious project was realized only gradually and with difficulties. In 1931 the building of the University of Chemistry and Technology was completed and before the outbreak of Second World War the joint building of the University of Architecture and Civil Engineering and the University of Agriculture and Forestry was also completed. The campus at Dejvice has been in construction for several generations now and undergoes continual transformations to adapt it to the needs of teaching and scientific research. The new buildings at the campus – for instance, the Faculty of Architecture, the new rectorate and the CIIRC (Czech Institute of Informatics, Robotics and Cybernetics) building – reflect the most modern world trends. In the first half of the 1960s the University of Agriculture moved from Dejvice to its own modern campus in Suchdol and is the only one of Prague's universities that has practical and theoretical teaching, student accommodation, administrative offices and all support services concentrated in one place.

The students' own May celebrations in Prague in 1965 took place in an atmosphere of a partial political thaw. A change of generations occurred 20 years after end of Second World War and students without their own harsh historical experience did not hesitate to subject totalitarianism to criticism and satire. In 1965 Prague students elected Allen Ginsberg as their king of May celebrations. Ginsberg, a nonconformist American poet, representative of the Beat Generation and an inspiration for the hippies, was expelled and deported from Czechoslovakia as a dangerous person who was allegedly corrupting socialist youth. This merely caused increased opposition to the totalitarian regime on the part of some of the students.

There has perhaps been no historical event that has taken place in the streets of Prague in the 20th century in which members of the academic community have not participated. In many of these events the academic community has played a leading role, while on more than one occasion members of the community have found themselves on opposite sides. In addition to events involving the whole of Czech society or the whole of Prague society, the universities have also experienced some events specific to the university context. For instance, in 1934 a dispute broke out between the German and Czech universities regarding the possession of the ancient insignia of Charles University. On 15 November 1939 a protest march took place in honour of medical student Jan Opletal, who had been fatally shot by German police during a demonstration to mark the anniversary of the foundation of the Czechoslovak Republic. Students from Charles University, the CTU, the Academy of Fine Arts and also UMPRUM took part in the protest march, and certainly none of them was able to imagine the extent of the repression that would be unleashed by the German powers just two days later: night raids at college halls of residence, executions,

Guard of honour at the coffin of 'living torch' student Jan Palach in the Karolinum courtyard on 25 January 1969. Jan Palach offered the ultimate sacrifice in order to arouse Czech society, which was beginning to reconcile itself with the occupation already half a year after the entry of the occupying armies.

internments in concentration camps and the closure of universities. In London in 1941, on the anniversary of this massacre, the 17th November was declared the International Day of Students, and the first international student congress took place in November 1945 in Prague. In reaction to the communist putsch in February 1948 some students reacted with a protest march on Prague Castle, while some left-inclined students seized membership in the action committees as the chance of a lifetime.

For the 40 years of Communist Party rule there was no room for public expressions of disagreement, but only for organized expressions of loyalty to the regime in May Day parades and celebrations of the Great October Socialist Revolution, in which pedagogues and students were obliged to take part. Already in the 1950s students made efforts to renew the historical tradition of their own May celebrations

Mourning procession at the funeral of Jan Palach on 25 January 1969, passing by the Philosophy Faculty of Charles University, where Palach studied.

and assembled on the eve of May 1 around the statue of Karel Hynek Mácha on Petřín hill. The tradition of a students' May Day celebration was only revived by a new generation in the 1960s: it took place until 1969 and was an opportunity for students to express their feelings about life through satire and jokes. However, even these officially permitted May parades were monitored by the State Security Service (StB) to ensure that criticism and irony did not go beyond a certain degree. In the opinion of the police bodies, this was exceeded, for instance, in 1967 by the protest march of the 'Strahovists' – students accommodated in the extremely sloppily built halls of residence at Strahov, where the electrical installations, water pipes and heating did not work properly. The brutal police intervention against the students was condemned by the entire Prague public. The atmosphere in this pre-spring of the Prague Spring had already changed markedly and other social groups also began gradually to come forward with expressions of dissatisfaction.

The hopes and plans of these groups for the future, as well as those of the universities, were extinguished by the arrival of the tanks of the Warsaw Pact armies in August 1968. The university's head office in Karolinum was occupied by Soviet

Students assembled at Albertov on 17 November 1989. From here they started an officially authorized march to commemorate the closure of universities in 1939 and to honour the International Day of Students.

17 November 1989, a few hours after the beginning of the peaceful demonstration. Students are sitting or kneeling on National Boulevard (Národní třída), divided from the police cordon by the state flag and holding flowers as a symbol of non-violence.

soldiers. In the autumn it seemed that the entire society was still united in its resistance to the occupiers. Prague students held a strike and occupied their faculties in protest against the occupation in November and again in December. Then they began to reconcile themselves gradually with the unchangeable reality, just as their parents did. This resignation out of tiredness was lit up by a living torch acting as a moral imperative – student Jan Palach. For a short time in January 1969 Palach's sacrifice acted as a moral imperative and moved the consciences of even the most indifferent. Fellow students and also academic officials bowed in respect before him, especially in the days around the funeral. However, after the April plenary session of the ruling party Palach's appeal shifted into the background amid the tangle of normalization compromises, checks carried out on staff members, and the everyday practical concerns of students and teachers. Nevertheless, this appeal was constantly present and once again motivated students 20 years later in the demonstrations during Palach's week in January 1989.

There is no need to recount the role played by students, primarily those from Prague, in the collapse of totalitarian power in November 1989, as this is not the past, but rather the beginning of our lived history. The events of 17 November 1989 opened a new era in the history of the country's universities and of the entire society. Following the fall of totalitarianism and the subsequent democratic changes university education developed to a hitherto unknown extent. Above all a network of regional universities was created; sometimes these successfully compete with the traditional universities in the big cities. In Prague itself there are dozens of private universities, which provide education and award titles in a wide range of subjects, even though in comparison with the state universities they play a fairly marginal role. In May 1990 Law no. 172 Coll. was passed: this guaranteed autonomy for universities by means of elected senates and scientific councils. Within the framework of the academic freedoms given by this law nine universities in Prague – eight public ones and one state one – are developing their activities. They educate roughly 110,000 students and award bachelor's, master's, engineer and doctorate titles to successful graduates.

For 670 years Prague has been proud to call itself a university town. The mutual co-existence of the metropolis and higher learning has been to the benefit of both. Universities make use of the hospitality of the capital city, which in turn is enriched architecturally, culturally, socially and demographically by the presence of the universities. Charles University, founded in 1348, has become rooted in the very heart of the city. However, over the centuries the tree of learning and higher education has spread so much that today, in search of university life, we have to journey not only to the city's historic quarters, but also to sections of the city on both the left and right banks of the Vltava that have been gradually incorporated in the capital city. Prague's university past is present in the names of the city's squares and streets; it has been inscribed in stone on monuments and memorials. Its present is taking place in both historic and new buildings, libraries, study centres and in the entire structure of the Czech metropolis.

We can see traces of the university's past or present in perhaps every Prague panorama. The massive building of the Lichtenstein Palace, which seems to arise directly from the surface of the Vltava river on the Kampa island not far from Charles Bridge, was used after 1869 by the Czech Polytechnic Institute of the Kingdom of Bohemia, the precursor of the Czech Technical University. →

PRAGUE: UNIVERSITY TOWN – AN ILLUSTRATED GUIDE

Ovocný trh 5 (Fruit Market)

Karolinum is the seat of Charles University's rectorate. The university has 17 faculties, of which 14 are located in Prague. Karolinum is a complex of mutually interconnected historical and modern buildings, which today are bounded by Celetná, Kamzíková, Železná streets and Ovocný trh. On the European continent Karolinum is the university building that has served without interruption the same purpose for the longest period of time: from its foundation until today it has been the main seat of the university. In the past the adjoining square was also named after the university: University Square, Royal Square, Karolinenplatz. The heart of Karolinum is Charles College, which was donated to Prague university by Wenceslas IV, the son of and successor to the university's founder Charles IV. In the years 1383–1386 he had the grand family home of the Rotlev family thoroughly reconstructed to serve the purposes of higher education. In particular he included sufficient space for assemblies of the university community – the aula – and an office for the rector, as well as establishing lecture halls, accommodation for masters and students, offices, a treasury, a library, a kitchen with a dining hall, storage rooms, a bathhouse and accommodation for staff. Karolinum has gone through good times and bad times, both in its academic significance and its architecture. Donations from supporters and benefactors enabled the university to pay the costs of internal decoration and facilities, but the maintenance of buildings was neglected for centuries resulting in walls and roofs falling into disrepair. The first substantial renovation started after 1600 and continued into the second half of the century. However, Karolinum only underwent a more thorough modernization in the years 1715–1718 with the Baroque reconstruction according to the plans of architect František Maxmilián Kaňka. It was only in the 1930s that the authorities of the Czechoslovak Republic showed an interest in Karolinum as a piece of heritage, but a general renovation was not actually carried out until the years 1945–1959. The current appearance of Karolinum is a testimonial to the sensitive and creative approach of architect Jaroslav Fragner, whose work was continued after 1990 by architect Tomáš Šantavý. Since 1963 Karolinum has been protected as a national monument.

The most pronounced feature of the Karolinum building is the Gothic oriel chapel with rich stone ornamentation. The chapel was a part of the original Rotlev Palace and sculptures representing masks of people and animals indicate that it was built in cooperation with the building workshop of master builder Petr Parléř. The coats-of-arms under the window belong to important figures of the time: the king of Bohemia and Queen Elizabeth, the Moravian margrave, the archbishop of Prague and finally the Rotlev family (a red lion). According to historians of art, the chapel's exterior was originally decorated with statues of patron saints of Bohemia – saints Wenceslas, Ludmila, Adalbert (Vojtěch), Vitus, Procopius (Prokop) and Sigismund (Zikmund).

A medieval timbered well in Karolinum's cellars belongs to an older structure from previous ages. Charles College had at its disposal water from a public fountain on New Market (today Fruit Market).

The cellar space of Karolinum reveals a much older ground-plan – apparently an early Gothic house structure which was here in the 13th and 14th centuries before the building of the Rotlev Palace. Charles University uses the space for storing and displaying historic items from the university's past. →

← The Gothic cross-vaulted cloister along Karolinum's south front was built on the ground floor in the 14th century in the course of the extension of the then banqueting hall on the first floor of the Rotlev Palace to create the Aula Magna of Charles College.

The ground-floor Gothic hall, originally the Maashaus of a former grandiose patrician mansion, is today used by Charles University for exhibitions and receptions. The hall was built in the place of the original arcades.

Gothic window in the reception area, the former Maashaus, with a view into the vaulted cloister. Medieval stone benches called *sedile* have also been preserved in several other places in Karolinum, for instance in the Aula Magna.

Bust of Milada Horáková (1901–1950), doctor of law and graduate of Charles University Law Faculty. A defender of democracy and freedom and an innocent victim of communist despotism, she was sentenced to death in a show-trial. The bust is the work of academic sculptor Věra Růžičková and was donated to Charles University by the Czech Society in Switzerland. It is located on the ground floor, where all visitors to the Aula Magna pass by it.

Imperial Hall on the ground floor of Karolinum as adapted by architect Tomáš Šantavý in 1997. It is named after the portraits of Marie Theresa and her sons Joseph II and Leopold II by Barbora Krafft-Steiner from 1799.

The marble memorial to Master Matouš Collinus z Chotěřiny (1516–1566), situated on the wall of the Aula Magna, is apparently the only Renaissance memorial left today at Karolinum. A pupil of Philipp Melanchton, Collinus (Kalina) was an outstanding humanist poet and man of learning and the first person to teach the Greek and Hebrew languages at Prague University. He recited Homer and introduced textbooks that were modern for the period. The memorial plaque was ordered out of gratitude by his protégé, Jacobus Palaeologus, a Greek monk living in exile. An alleged progeny of the Byzantine emperors, Palaeologus was later burned at the stake in Rome as a heretic. The plaque, intended for the Aula Magna, was for many years displayed in Karolinum's courtyard, but it is not a gravestone. Master Collinus was buried in the Bethlehem Chapel.

Baroque portal – entrance to the Aula Magna.

The Aula Magna, which for centuries has been the venue of important and ceremonial occasions in the life of the entire academic community and its individual members, is today much more spacious than it was in the past. It acquired a high ceiling during Baroque alterations. The post-war reconstruction extended its length by one third by incorporating a former lecture hall of the Law Faculty. The architect moved the head of the hall to its newly incorporated part and had a large tapestry, woven with the university's symbols, hung on this. The hall features an undulating suspended ceiling in the form of a baldachin with the silver symbols of the Lands of the Bohemian Crown by Jan Lauda. The hall has an excellent lighting system and superb acoustics. It was unveiled in this form for the first time in 1948 on the occasion of the 600th anniversary of the founding of Prague University.

The bronze statue of Charles IV by Karel Pokorný (1950) lends an air of monumentality to the ceremonial platform.

Oriel of the Aula Magna with a copy of the Gothic altar from Dubňany near Litoměřice, which is a work of a Bohemian master from the period around 1460. The original altar was brought to the oriel chapel in 1950 and a copy of it was made in 2004 by Jaroslav Alt. The altar's panel depicts a crowned Madonna in the centre with the holy patrons Barbara and Catherine on the side panels. The stained glass windows of the chapel in the neo-Gothic style were designed by builder and restorer Josef Mocker.

A tapestry with dimensions of 500 × 745 cm and containing the university's symbols, woven by Marie Teinitzerová according to a design by Vladimír Sychra (1947), covers the front wall of Karolinum's Aula Magna. The motif of the university seal, in which Charles IV entrusts university higher learning to the protection of the holy patron Prince Wenceslas, is surrounded by heraldic symbols and symbols of the four original university faculties: Medical Faculty – a pelican feeding its young with its own blood; Philosophy Faculty – the Earth and the heavenly bodies; Law Faculty – scales of justice; Theology Faculty – an eagle flying toward the sun.

PER ALIENA
PARATAM IN
IONIS

V.JYCHRA 1997

Karel Škréta: Saint John the Evangelist, 1750, oil on canvas, 232.2 × 143.3 cm. The patron of theologians is here depicted on the island of Patmos while writing the Book of the Revelations (Apocalypse). Originally the portrait hung in the Aula Magna opposite a portrait of St. Catherine, but now both pictures are in the Karolinum Gallery.

Karel Škréta: Saint Catherine, 1658, oil on canvas,
231.5 × 142 cm. The patron of philosophers is surrounded
by the attributes of learning and instruments of knowledge.
The painting by the famous Czech Baroque master was
donated to the university by the later Polish King Michał
Wiśniowecki.

Hall of Patriots, in which from 1784 onwards patriots of the
Royal Bohemian Society of Sciences met for councils and in
which they had a library. The hall was modified in 1997, when
the casts of six busts of significant Czech men of learning
from the period of the National Revival were placed between
the windows. The walls feature paintings by Antonín Machek.
The unique knotted carpet from 1924 depicts a symbolic map
of Bohemia.

Portrait of President T. G. Masaryk by Otto Peters from 1932
(oil on canvas, 188 × 103 cm). This was originally intended
for the front of the Aula Magna, but today it is located in the
Hall of Patriots.

The current Aula Minor on the first floor of Karolinum was at one time the main lecture hall of the Medical Faculty. This is recalled by the portraits of important professors of medicine on the walls and a painting by Johann Georg Heinsch of Saints Cosmas and Damian Healing the Sick (1698) on the front wall. The Aula Minor played a significant role in university life, as the elections of Prague university's rectors took place here.

The medieval plan of the entire complex has remained
preserved as a result of retaining the original central
courtyard, in which important assemblies in the history
of both the university and of Prague have taken place.

The historical continuity is also emphasized by the statue of Master Jan Hus by Karel Lidický (1957) located in the courtyard where in 1409 Hus's election as rector was accompanied by excited voices and where seven years later the signatories of a protest against the burning at stake of two members of the university community – Jan Hus and Jerome of Prague – held a solemn procession. It was under Hus's statue that on 25 January 1969 the academic community symbolically paid its last respects to Jan Palach.

The façade of Karolinum facing Železná Street, which before Fragner's reconstruction was still the main entrance until the middle of the last century. The sandstone portal of the doors and the segmental balcony were built by F. M. Kaňka in the years 1715–1718.

2A–C/ FACULTY OF ARTS
Náměstí Jana Palacha (Jan Palach Square)
The dean's office of the Faculty of Arts (Philosophy Faculty)
is located in its main building, which was built according to
a design by Josef Sakař in 1930. The faculty is one of the four
original faculties which constituted Prague universal higher
learning at the time of its foundation in the 14th century.
At that time the faculty was called the faculty of the seven
liberal arts (or arts faculty) and it had the greatest number of
students and pedagogues. Since the middle of the 17th century
the faculty has been based at Klementinum and its program
of study has been enriched by newly emerging natural
scientific and technical disciplines.

Bronze memorial plaque to Jan Palach, a student at the faculty, with a relief portrait sculpted by Olbram Zoubek according to Palach's funeral mask and with a Czech heraldic lion, located to the left of the building's portico. The date 16 January 1969 recalls the day of Palach's self-sacrifice.

Statue of T. G. Masaryk, located in a niche at the front of the main staircase, by Jan Štursa. After the division of Charles-Ferdinand University into a Czech and a German university in 1882, Masaryk was appointed an extraordinary professor of philosophy at this faculty and from 1897 until the First World War he was a regular professor. The statue was placed here in 1945, it was removed in the 1950s, in 1968 it was installed once again for a short time, and it has stood here permanently since 1990.

3A–C/ FACULTY OF LAW
Náměstí Curieových 7 (Curies Square)
The building of the dean's office of the Faculty of Law was
built in the years 1924–1931 to a design by Jan Kotěra, one
of the creators of Czech modernism. The building, which was
completed by Ladislav Machoň, is one of the most interesting
monumental buildings from the 1920s in Prague. Many of the
original decorative arts-and-crafts details have been preserved
in the building's interiors. The Law Faculty was one of the
four original faculties at the university's foundation.

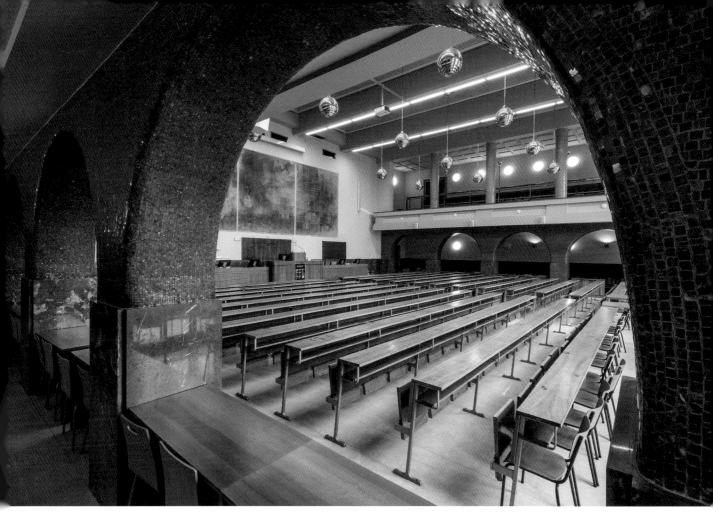

The central vestibule of the Faculty, a three-storey rectangular space with granite tiles on the ground floor, surrounded by galleries on pillars and covered by a glass ceiling with a metal truss construction.

The Aula Maxima of the Faculty of Law, which during the period of Karolinum's reconstruction was used temporarily as a common assembly room and as a hall for graduation ceremonies instead of the Aula Magna at Karolinum.

4/ FACULTY OF EDUCATION

M. D. Rettigové 4

The dean's office of the Faculty of Education is situated in the building of the former Eliška Krásnohorská town grammar school for girls, originally built in 1882 and later reconstructed in the functionalist style. The faculty was established in 1946 as the sixth university faculty. In 1955 it was granted independent status as the Pedagogical University, but in 1964 it reverted to the status of a university faculty. It trains teachers and pedagogical specialists at all levels of schooling. The faculty has used the building in Rettigová Street since 1948. Some teaching takes place in the town of Brandýs nad Labem (30 km northeast of Prague).

5/ FACULTY OF SCIENCE

5A–B/
Albertov 6
The dean's office of the Faculty of Science is situated in one
of the buildings in the Albertov complex, which was built
gradually for the university from the end of the 19th century
onwards. Several other institutes belonging to the faculty
are located in the vicinity: the geological, geographical,
biological and chemical institutes. This building entered the
history of the university and also that of Prague primarily in
relation to two November demonstrations that started here:
the protest march on 15 November 1939 following the death
of student Jan Opletal and the march on 17 November 1989
to commemorate the closure of Czech universities by the
Nazis. The 1989 march ended in a massacre at Národní třída
(National Boulevard). The Faculty of Science was established
in 1920. Until that time natural scientific disciplines, including
mathematics and physics, had been taught at the Philosophy
Faculty. During the 20th century the diversification and
development of the natural scientific disciplines proceeded
at such a pace that already in the 1950s a further division
occurred. In 1953 the Faculty of Science was firstly formally
divided into three faculties: a geological-geographical
faculty, a mathematical-physical faculty and a biological
faculty. In 1959 the geological-geographical faculty and the
biological faculty were merged into one faculty, which also
included the study of chemistry. The faculty owns several
valuable collections: for instance, the Hrdlička Museum
of Anthropology, the Mineralogical Museum and the map
collection. The botanical garden also belongs to the faculty.

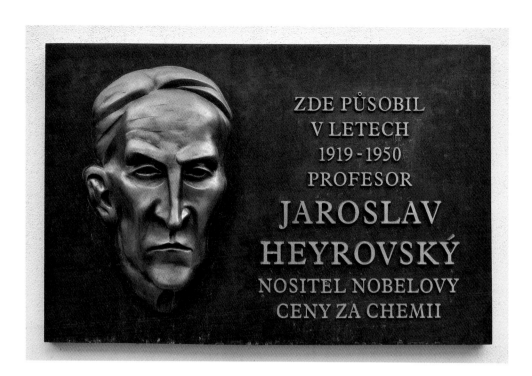

ZDE PŮSOBIL
V LETECH
1919 - 1950
PROFESOR
JAROSLAV
HEYROVSKÝ
NOSITEL NOBELOVY
CENY ZA CHEMII

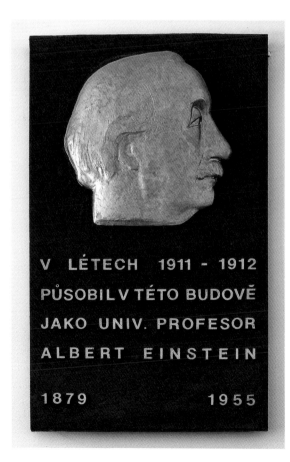

V LÉTECH 1911 - 1912
PŮSOBIL V TÉTO BUDOVĚ
JAKO UNIV. PROFESOR
ALBERT EINSTEIN
1879   1955

5C/

In 1922 Jaroslav Heyrovský became the first professor of physical chemistry at the Faculty of Natural Sciences. In 1959 he received the Nobel Prize for Chemistry for his discovery of the polarograph and the analytical method of polarography. The commemorative plaque on the building of the Chemical Institute at Albertov is one of four plaques in the streets of Prague that recall Heyrovský's achievements.

5D/

Viničná 7

A bronze relief with the profile of Albert Einstein located in the vestibule of the building of the former German university's Natural Sciences Institute recalls that the still young scientist lectured here in the years 1911–1912 at the newly established Institute of Theoretical Physics.

5E–F/
Benátská 2

The university's botanical garden was founded in 1775 by
Josef Bohumír Mikan in the Smíchov district of Prague. It was
moved to the New Town in 1898, when the botanical gardens
and greenhouses of both Charles-Ferdinand universities, the
Czech and German entities, were transferred to the former
gardens of the Society for the Promotion of Gardening (also
known as the Social Gardens or Federal Gardens). The garden
has an area of 3.5 hectares and is open to the public.

6/ FACULTY OF MATHEMATICS AND PHYSICS

6A/

Ke Karlovu 3

The Faculty of Mathematics and Physics was established
in 1952 as the seventh university faculty when it was given
independent status from the Faculty of Natural Sciences.
The current seat of the faculty's dean's office was built as
the Mathematics and Natural Sciences Institute of Charles
University in 1907 in connection with the construction of the
neighbouring Physics Institute. Up until 1920 both disciplines
were taught at the Philosophy Faculty and in the years
1920–1952 at the Faculty of Natural Sciences. In addition to
the building of the dean's office in the Karlov area, the faculty
also owns other buildings in the Lesser and New Town,
and in the Karlín, Troja and Hostivař districts.

6B–E/

Malostranské náměstí 25 (Lesser Town Square)
In 1960 the Faculty of Mathematics and Physics acquired
teaching and office space in the former Jesuit professed house
on the Lesser Town Square, an early Baroque building from
the years 1614–1691, built by Giovanni Domenico Orsi and
Francesco Lurago. In 2006, after an exacting reconstruction,
a conference and social centre was opened here. The faculty
uses the building primarily for the teaching of information
technology.

Since 2008, following its repair, the architecturally valuable former refectory has been used as an aula for bachelor's degree graduation ceremonies of Charles University, as well as concerts and ceremonial assemblies.

In 2003, during a reconstruction carried out by the Faculty of Mathematics and Physics, remains of the rotunda of St. Wenceslas from the 10th century were uncovered. It had been thought that this rotunda had been destroyed during the building's Baroque reconstruction. The rescue of this historic building and making it accessible for the public took place in the years 2014–2015 within the framework of an IMF project, co-financed from EU funds for the protection of cultural heritage and Norwegian funds. A valuable find was the original floor of the rotunda with terracotta tiles.

The Rotunda computer laboratory. →

6F/

V Holešovičkách 2

The development and diversification of the physical sciences after Second World War, especially in the field of nuclear physics, led to deliberations about mutual cooperation between the Faculty of Mathematics and Physics at Charles University and the Faculty of Theoretical and Nuclear Physics at the Czech Technical University in Prague. In 1968, within the framework of these plans, work started on the construction of a new mathematical physics workplace in Prague 8 district (Pelc-Tyrolka). Construction was completed in 1978 and some disciplines in the fields of physics and astronomy, as well as laboratories and workshops, were moved to the site. During the following ten years new student halls
of residence were also opened here.

7A/

Kateřinská 32

The Medical Faculty is one of the four original faculties that formed a part of Prague higher learning at the time of the university's foundation. It is thus the oldest medical faculty in central Europe, even though the medieval conception of medical study was far removed from the current-day conception. For instance, it was only after several centuries that the fields of surgery and obstetrics came to be regarded as part of medical studies. After an independent medical faculty specializing in paediatrics and public health was established in 1953, the direct successor of the original Medical Faculty was renamed the Faculty of General Medicine. This newly named faculty covered teaching, research and clinics in a wide spectrum of specializations and it inherited the existing buildings of the original faculty. The address of the dean's office in Kateřinská (Catherine) Street recalls the existence of an institute for the insane, established here after the abolition of the convent of Augustinian nuns at St. Catherine in the 18th century.

7B/

Karlovo náměstí (Charles Square) 36

The early Baroque college of the New Town Jesuits is the largest Baroque building in Prague's New Town. It was built according to plans by Carlo Lurago and Martin Reiner in the years 1658–1759. Following the abolition of the Jesuit order in 1773 a military hospital was established here. The building, which has undergone many alterations, has been used as a hospital ever since then and today it is a part of the General Medical Faculty Hospital.

Karlovo náměstí (Charles Square) 40
The Mladota Palace, also known as the Faust House,
with its Gothic core and Renaissance and Baroque
alterations, is an example of the significant phenomenon
of Prague mythology. In the 16th century it was owned
by Edward Kelly, the court alchemist of Rudolph II, and
in the 18th century Ferdinand Antonín Mladota, a knight
from Solopysk, carried out his chemical and physical
experiments here. This is perhaps the origin of the tale
about Doctor Faust, the devil and the irreparable hole in
the ceiling. From 1838 the building served as an institute
for the deaf and dumb and in 1902 it was purchased by the
neighbouring General Medical Faculty Hospital. Today it
is used by the First Faculty of Medicine for social events.

7D/

Apolinářská 18

The Royal Bohemian Maternity Ward at St. Apollinaire, as it
was called at the time of its foundation, was built in the years
1865–1875 in the neo-Gothic style according to a design by
Josef Hlávka. Its construction was prompted by the transfer
of the previous hospital for foundlings, which included a
maternity ward, from the hands of the congregation of St.
Apollinaire Church to state administration. The maternity
ward was the seat of the maternity wards of both the Czech
and German universities and it continues to serve as a
teaching post of the Medical Faculty to this day.

8/ SECOND FACULTY OF MEDICINE
V Úvalu 84

After 1989 the then Faculty of Paediatrics moved to a complex of faculty and hospital buildings at Motol, where it gradually concentrated all its clinics and theoretical facilities. Construction of the complex began in 1964. The 13-storey bloc containing the dean's office of the faculty and a children's hospital was completed in 1970. Today the specialization in paediatrics is evident primarily in the clinical field, but doctors in all areas of medicine are trained here.

9/ THIRD FACULTY OF MEDICINE
Ruská 87

The building of the dean's office and the institutes of the Third
Faculty of Medicine in the Královské Vinohrady district. The
faculty is the successor institution to the Faculty of Public
Health, which was established as part of the reorganization
and decentralization of medical fields in 1953. Hospital
doctors are trained in various specialisms at the faculty, while
its one-time specialization is reflected in particular in its
cooperation with the State Public Health Institute.

10A–D/ CATHOLIC THEOLOGICAL FACULTY

Thákurova 3

The Catholic Theological Faculty, one of the four oldest faculties of the entire Charles University, has been located in the building of the Archbishop's Seminary in Prague's Dejvice district since 1928, though with some enforced interruptions. The period 1939–1945 was not the only one of these. During the years of the socialist experiment the faculty was formally expelled from the university, even though the legal and factual continuity are not in doubt. In 1953 it had to leave the building in Dejvice and relocate temporarily to a former institute for the deaf and dumb in the town of Litoměřice. The ceremonial return of the faculty to the university took place in September 1990. The faculty educates Catholic priests, historians of Christian art and also lay workers of church and charitable institutions.

The seminary's refectory.

← The high and spacious internal chapel on the highest floor
under a central cupola also serves as the faculty's aula.

11/ PROTESTANT THEOLOGICAL FACULTY

Černá 9

The Protestant Theological Faculty, incorporated into Charles University in 1990, is a successor to the Czechoslovak Hussite Protestant Theological Faculty, established in 1919, the name of which was changed in 1950 to the Comenius Protestant Theological Faculty. The dean's office of the faculty in Černá Street, originally built in 1927 for the Plicht Physical Education Institute, was purchased for the faculty and adapted for its use in the 1990s. Up until 1995 the faculty was located in the Hus House (Husův dům) on Jungmannova Street.

12/ HUSSITE THEOLOGICAL FACULTY
Pacovská 350
The dean's office of the Hussite Theological Faculty. The faculty, established in 1990 and originally located in the building of the Jan Hus Congregation Church in Dejvice in the Prague 6 district, teaches Hussite and Orthodox theology, but also offers broader education in the humanities.

13/ FACULTY OF SOCIAL SCIENCES
Smetanovo nábřeží 6

The faculty was established in 1990, but carries on the work of university teaching in the field of the social sciences and media and in particular the work of the independent Faculty of Journalism, which operated in the years 1972–1990. The current faculty also offers a broad range of education in the fields of economics, politics and international relations. The dean's office is situated in an historic building from 1846 called the Hollar House, but most teaching takes place in the new university complex in the district of Jinonice.

14/ FACULTY OF HUMANITIES
U Kříže 8

Charles University's youngest faculty was established in 2000
as a successor to the Institute of the Foundations of Culture,
which was a joint project of the university and the Czech
Academy of Sciences in the years 1990–1999. It is based at
a modern complex of Charles University at Jinonice, which
the university took over, in a half-built condition, from the
Ministry of Education, Youth and Physical Education in 1999.
Today the Faculty of Arts and the Faculty of Social Sciences
also have lecture halls at the complex.

15/ FACULTY OF PHYSICAL EDUCATION AND SPORT

José Martího 31

The Faculty of Physical Education and Sport was incorporated into the university in 1965 and continued the work of the preceding Institute of Physical Education and Sport. The institute was set up in 1953 and was given the use of the Tyrš House (Tyršův Dům) in the Lesser Town, which was the property of the Czechoslovak Sokol gymnastics organization. In 1990, when the property was returned to its legal owner, the faculty moved to a building of the abolished University of Politics of the Central Committee of the Czechoslovak Communist Party in the Veleslavín district, originally built by architect Pavel Bareš in the years 1949–1953 as a school for the National Security Service.

16A–G/ KLEMENTINUM

Křižovnická 2

The façade and main entrance to Klementinum (Clementinum) from Mariánské náměstí (Marian Square). Klementinum is named after the older Church of St. Clement and is one of the Baroque jewels of Prague. The oldest and most extensive college in Bohemia was conceived by the Jesuits in a truly grandiose fashion and they entrusted its construction to some of the foremost architects and artists of the period. The complex, which consists of a group of buildings and courtyards, contains both teaching and accommodation premises, a library, two churches and three chapels. Building was begun by Carlo Lurago in 1653, but was only completed at the beginning of the 18th century. After the merger of Karolinum and Klementinum in 1654 to form the new Charles-Ferdinand University, the philosophical and theological faculties were based here. After the abolition of the Jesuit order, the Philosophy Faculty had sufficient space to be able to develop the teaching of natural sciences here and also to provide instruction in the newly demanded technical and agricultural fields of study. After its foundation, the Academy of Fine Arts was also based here. Later Charles University used Klementinum primarily for its extensive university library, which is today a part of the National Library of the Czech Republic.

Baroque library hall. →

← Klementinum's summer refectory with rich stucco decoration from the period before 1680 is used as a general study room.

The memorial to the students who, under the leadership of Jesuit Jiří Plachý, defended the Old Town bridge tower against the Swedes in 1648 was sculpted in 1847 by Viennese sculptor Josef Max to celebrate the 200th anniversary of the battle.

The quad of the former Jesuit College, its oldest part, today called Vine Court (Révové nádvoří).

Astronomical tower of the central wing, built before 1722. As a dominant feature of the entire complex it was originally open to the sky. The onion dome, with a statue of Atlas from the workshop of Mathias Bernard Braun, was only added later.

The Church of the Holy Saviour dominates the rear façade of the Klementinum complex as seen from Charles Bridge. It was built as a three-aisle church on the foundations of the former Church of St. Clement from 1578. The gable and gallery on the façade bear 14 sandstone statues from the workshop of Jan Jiří Bendl from the years 1655–1660. An Immaculata (Immaculate Virgin Mary) is placed in a niche in the middle, surrounded by the figures of Christ, the evangelists, the Jesuit saints and the church fathers. As a part of Klementinum the church served the Jesuit College and, after its merger with the university in 1654, the entire academic community. Outstanding university professors, such as Bernard Bolzano, preached from the pulpit here. In 1990 the connection with the university was renewed and the church became an assembly place for students of the Roman Catholic faith. In 2004 a parish was directly established here for the pastoral care of university students, pedagogues and their families. The church is also used for concerts of church music.

17/ LUSATIAN SEMINARY

U Lužického semináře 13

The Lusatian Seminary was founded in 1724 as a college for students from Upper Lusatia, who prepared to become Roman Catholic priests here. It was intended as an assistance to the Lusatian diocese in countering continuing Germanization and Protestantization in Saxony. The seminary had a high cultural level and its graduates significantly influenced the Lusatian national revival. In 1922, when the seminary was abolished, it had 21 students. The building, built in the years 1726–1728 according to the plans of Kilian Ignaz Dientzenhofer, once again served its original purpose in the years 1945–1955. It is currently used by the Ministry of Education, Youth and Physical Education and also by the Society of Friends of Lusatia, which operates a valuable library that bears the name of Lusatian patriot Michal Hórnik.

18/ STRAHOV HALLS OF RESIDENCE
Vaníčkova 7

The Strahov halls of residence were built in the years 1964–1965 near to the large Strahov stadium as occasional accommodation for gymnasts taking part in the Spartakiads. The mass gymnastic performances known as the Spartakiads took place every five years in the years 1955–1985 and carried on the tradition of the former famous Sokol gymnastics meetings. Today the Strahov halls of residence are used by students of the Czech Technical University.

19A/

Jugoslávských partyzánů 3

The Czech Technical University (CTU) is the third largest university in Prague and is one of the oldest technical universities in Europe. At the current time it is comprised of eight faculties: the Faculty of Civil Engineering, the Faculty of Mechanical Engineering, the Faculty of Electrical Engineering, the Nuclear Sciences and Physical Engineering Faculty, the Faculty of Architecture, the Faculty of Transportation Sciences, the Faculty of Biomedical Engineering and the Faculty of Information Technology. The youngest part of the CTU is the Czech Institute of Informatics, Robotics and Cybernetics (CIIRC), which was founded in 2013. The CIIRC's noteworthy building, designed by architect Petr Franta and his team, was completed in 2017, when it also became the new home of the rectorate of the entire CTU.

19B–C/

Karlovo náměstí 13

The neo-Renaissance building of the Czech Technical
University, the former Czech Polytechnic, was built according
to a design by Ignác Ullman in the years 1871–1875 and for
a considerable time had to deal with problems of insufficient
space for rapidly developing disciplines. The polytechnic
also had use of a neighbouring building in Resslova Street,
a former house for emeritus priests, which Ignác Ullmann
modified in 1871 so as to make it possible to use the building
for teaching. A noteworthy architectural feature of the new
building is the ground-floor vestibule, which opens onto a
semi-circular stairway.

19D/

Husova 5

From the year 1786 until the 1980s technical subjects were taught in the building of the Bohemian Estates Engineering School on the premises of the former St. Wenceslas Seminary, which was altered in the Baroque style at the turn of the 17th and 18th centuries. On 10 November 1806 in the large lecture hall here Professor František Josef Gerstner ceremonially initiated teaching at the Royal Bohemian Estates Technical Institute – Prague Polytechnic.

19E/

Konviktská 22

The building, which today is used by the Faculty of Transportation Sciences, was built according to plans by Victor Beneš in 1901 for the German Polytechnic – that is, the K. k. Deutsche Technische Hochschule in Prag (Imperial and Royal German Technical University in Prague). The Faculty of Transportation Sciences also has teaching premises in the Albertov complex.

19F/

Břehová 7

The building of the Faculty of Nuclear Sciences and Physical Engineering in Břehová Street was transferred to the CTU in the 1950s together with the former Faculty of Technology and Nuclear Physics at Charles University. This was established at Charles University in 1955 at a time of rapid development in nuclear physics after Second World War. However, the limitations of purely theoretical study in mathematical physics soon became apparent. The study of nuclear physics and technology necessarily required the connection of theoretical study in natural scientific disciplines with practical experience in technology and engineering. Therefore, in 1959 the faculty was transferred to the CTU and given its current-day name. The building, built by Josef Sakař in the years 1920–1922, was first used by the Ministry of Foreign Trade of the Czechoslovak Republic, then temporarily by the Philosophy Faculty of Charles University, and then by the Faculty of Nuclear Sciences.

19G/

Thákurova 9

This new CTU building, occupied by the Faculty of
Architecture and the Faculty of Information Technology, was
opened in 2011. The project by architect Alena Šrámková
and her team is another in a series of successful attempts to
extend the Dejvice technical studies campus. The Faculty of
Architecture is situated next to the Faculty of Construction,
which gained independent status in 1976. A corridor on the
first floor connects the buildings of the two faculties, which
complement each other in their study programs.

Betlémské náměstí 4

The Bethlehem Chapel, the most significant pre-Hussite assembly place of Prague University and also a forum for university masters to spread their ideas among the town public, was built in 1394 as a simple, spacious building with a wooden ceiling on a trapezoidal ground-plan. A vault was added in the 16th century, when the church was regarded by Prague burghers as a memorial to Jan Hus, who preached here in the years 1402–1413. At the end of the 18th century the dilapidated chapel was in danger of collapse and some town houses were built among its ruins. The current form of the chapel is thus actually a new building from the years 1950–1952 – a reconstruction according to old drawings and historical-architectural research, which was designed by architect Jaroslav Fragner. Today the Chapel of the Bethlehem Innocents, known in short as the Bethlehem Chapel, serves the CTU as a ceremonial venue, where assemblies, concerts and graduation ceremonies are held.

19H/
Zikova 4 / Šolínova 7

The Klokner Institute was founded in 1921 by Professor František Klokner as the Institute of Building Materials and Building Structures. At that time it was the only institute of its kind in Czechoslovakia and also in central Europe, and it became part of the CTU as an independent department. It is located in a building that was originally intended for the Faculty of Agriculture and Forestry Science and which was built in the years 1929–1937 according to a project by Antonín Engel and Theodor Petřík. Engel's ambitious project, conceived in the 1920s, was aimed at providing all the universities associated in the CTU, including their rectorates, with their own buildings within the Dejvice complex. However, construction proceeded slowly and the faculties had to lower their expectations. The Klokner Institute moved into the completed building, which until very recently it shared with the CTU's central rectorate.

20/ ACADEMY OF FINE ARTS

20A/
U Akademie 2
The Academy of Fine Arts (AVU) is the oldest artistic university in Prague. It was founded in 1799 and its activities have influenced the creative atmosphere and artistic form of the city for two centuries. The university's rectorate is located in an Art Nouveau building designed by Václav Roštlapil and built in the years 1897–1903. The university does not have faculties, but provides instruction in individual ateliers.

20 B/

U Akademie 4

The School of Architecture, the architecture atelier and the
new-media atelier are located next to the main AVU building.
The building, designed by Jan Kotěra and Josef Gočár, was
built in the years 1922–1924.

20 C–D/

U Starého výstaviště 188 (Výstaviště 188)

The Modern Gallery building was built by architect Antonín
Wiehl for the General Land Centennial Exhibition held in
Prague in 1891. The academy gained temporary use of the
building immediately after the end of the exhibition, but
only acquired it permanently in 1945. The building, which
was renovated in 2003, houses graphic art studios and ateliers
devoted to restoration work.

20E/

Slovenská 4

AVU acquired the Šaloun atelier in the Vinohrady district in 2001 in an extremely dilapidated state. After a costly reconstruction, which the academy carried out in the years 2006–2007, it is now registered as a cultural monument. The atelier, like the Šaloun Villa and the adjoining garden, was built between 1908 and 1911 according to a design by sculptor Ladislav Šaloun for his own use, apparently after he had won the competition for a memorial to Jan Hus on the Old Town Square. The atelier now houses a gallery of Šaloun's sculptures and also serves as teaching space.

náměstí Jana Palacha 3

The Academy of Arts, Architecture & Design (AAAD),
generally known as UMPRUM (University of Decorative
Arts), is situated in a building from 1882, which was designed
for it by Jan Machytka and František Schmoranz Jr., who also
become its first director in 1885. The academy only gained
the legal status of a university in 1946, but long before that
it had already represented Czech art in a dignified way, in
particular as one of the centres of applied arts and the Art
Nouveau movement at the turn of the 20th century. The school
teaches theoretical subjects in six departments and provides
instruction in artistic creation in more than 20 ateliers.

Memorial plaque from 1924 to architect Jan Kotěra
(1871–1923), a professor at UMPRUM (AAAD), on the
building's main façade.

Ateliers at UMPRUM (AAAD).

22A–B/
Malostranské náměstí (Lesser Town Square) 12–13
The Academy of Performing Arts (AMU) was founded in 1945
and began teaching in the academic year 1946/47. In the 70
years of its operation it has had a significant impact on Czech
culture and the artistic environment of Prague. It teaches
subjects in the fields of theatre, film, music and dance. It has
three faculties: the Theatre Faculty (DAMU), the Film and
TV Faculty (FAMU) and the Music and Dance Faculty
(HAMU). The academy's rectorate is situated in the
Hartig Palace in the Lesser Town and is connected with
the Lichtenstein Palace, which is used by HAMU. The
Lichtenstein Palace is an imposing building which – behind
a unifying classicist façade from the end of the 18th century –
conceals the remains of several patrician and noble houses
from the Gothic and Renaissance eras. The most opulent room
in the palace is the large concert hall on the first floor named
after composer Bohuslav Martinů. All three faculties of AMU
use the concert hall for graduation ceremonies.

Studio of AMU's Music Faculty.

22C–D/
Karlova 26
AMU's Theatre Faculty is situated behind the High-Baroque
façade of an inconspicuous house, historically called the
Kokořovský Palace. The building's inspirational interior,
which was created by connecting two buildings, comprises
a variety of different spaces. The building contains the dean's
office, lecture halls and the faculty's own theatre, the famous
DISK.

Hall of the DISK theatre.

22E/

Smetanovo nábřeží 2

At its foundation in 1945 the Film and TV Faculty (FAMU)
obviously did not have 'television' in its name, as the first
attempts at television only happened eight years later. It was
only in the mid 1060s, when film makers became interested
in the potential of television broadcasting, that the word
television was added to the faculty's name. At the time of
its foundation it was only the fifth university of film in the
whole world and it quickly gained respect. Since the 1960/61
academic year its dean's office and teaching premises have
been located in the Lažanský Palace, designed by architect
Ignác Ullmann and built in the years 1861–1863. The Slavia
Café on the ground floor does not belong to the university,
but FAMU has its own student club in the building's historic
cellars. The FAMU Studio in Klimentská Street is also part
of the faculty.

23A–B/
Kamýcká 129

The Czech University of Life Sciences (CULS) was the first
of Prague's universities to obtain a modern campus which
provides the entire range of its needs: administration and
teaching premises, as well as halls of residence. It moved
to the Suchdol complex in the mid-1960s, when it was
still called the University of Agriculture, from the Dejvice
complex, where the schools associated in the Czech Technical
University (CTU) had a common location. From 1920 until
1952 the University of Agriculture and Forestry Science was
also a part of the CTU. The CULS rectorate manages six
faculties: the Faculty of Economics and Management, the
Faculty of Agrobiology, Food and Natural Resources, the
Faculty of Engineering, the Faculty of Forestry and Wood
Sciences, the Faculty of Environmental Sciences and the
Faculty of Tropical AgriSciences. The university also has two
workplaces outside of Prague: in Lány and Kostelec nad
Černými Lesy. It is currently the second largest university in
Prague.

The pleasure garden in the CULS complex with an area
of 2.67 hectares is open to the public. It serves for the
development of teaching and research in the field of garden
and landscape architecture. Hundreds of different types of
trees and perennials are planted here. →

23C/
Kamýcká 1176
The building of the CULS's Faculty of Forestry and Wood
Sciences with its tree logo.

23D/
Havlíčkovy sady 58
The Grébovka (Gröbovka) Villa built in the years 1871–1888,
surrounded by an English park. The University of Agriculture
and Forestry Sciences, as part of the CTU, was located here
in the years 1920–1936. Today the building is registered as
a Prague cultural monument.

24/ UNIVERSITY OF CHEMISTRY
AND TECHNOLOGY, PRAGUE
Technická 5

There is a more-than-200-year tradition of the teaching of chemistry in Prague. This tradition reaches back to the very beginnings of the Prague Polytechnic, which was a historical predecessor of the University of Chemistry and Technology. In the years 1920–1939, as the University of Chemistry and Technical Engineering, it was a part of the group of universities associated in the CTU. After 1945 it was CTU's Faculty of Chemistry and in 1952 it regained the status of an independent university with its current name. It continues to be located in the Dejvice complex, which it shares with the CTU. It has played a significant role in the modernization of industrial technologies and it is one of Europe's foremost universities in a range of specializations. It has four faculties: the Faculty of Chemical Technology, the Faculty of Environmental Technology, the Faculty of Food and Biochemical Technology and the Faculty of Chemical Engineering. Individual faculties are divided into departments, of which there are a total of 29.

25A–C/ UNIVERSITY OF ECONOMICS, PRAGUE
W. Churchilla 4 / U Rajské zahrady 3
Currently the fourth largest university in Prague, the University of Economics was founded in 1953. Apart from its main premises at a complex in the Žižkov district of Prague, which is growing in accord with the growth of the university's significance, it also has three more complexes with halls of residence in Prague. The rectorate, which is located in the so-called Old Building, manages six faculties, five of which are located in the capital city and one in Jindřichův Hradec (South Bohemia). These are: the Faculty of Finance and Accounting, the Faculty of International Relations, the Faculty of Business Administration, the Faculty of Informatics and Statistics, the Faculty of Economics and the Faculty of Management.

The interior of the new building, known as the Rajská (Paradise) Building after the name of the garden area which previously occupied the site. The building has seven floors and was opened in 2005.

The Vencovský Aula, the university's largest lecture hall. It was originally called the New Aula, but was renamed in 2008 in honour of Professor František Vencovský, an important economist and historian of economic thought.

26/ POLICE ACADEMY OF CZECH REPUBLIC IN PRAGUE

Lhotecká 7

The youngest university in Prague is the Police Academy of the Czech Republic, founded in 1993. In comparison with the eight other universities in Prague it has a somewhat different standing: it is an organizational unit of the Interior Ministry. Its rectorate and teaching premises are located in a modern complex in the vicinity of Prague's Modřany district, where the university also has its own aula. It is comprised of two faculties: the Faculty of Security Law and the Faculty of Security Management. The university's aim is to educate experts for specialized professions in the security services, both in the private and public sectors.

27A–B/ NATIONAL LIBRARY OF TECHNOLOGY
Technická 6

In 2009 the National Library of Technology was opened
in the Dejvice complex occupied by technical universities.
It contains more than 1.5 million volumes. Many of these
were originally located at Klementinum, where the fund of
technical literature was built up over many years along with
the historical development of the technical subjects taught
there. The cleverly designed and architecturally noteworthy
nine-storey building with a rounded-square ground plan,
which only took two years to build, is the work of the
Projektil architects studio. The drawings on the concrete walls
of the galleries of the spacious atria are the work of Romanian
artist Dan Perjovschi.

NUMBER OF UNIVERSITY STUDENTS IN PRAGUE

Charles University – 49,236
Czech University of Life Sciences – 19,940
Czech Technical University – 19,102
University of Economics – 14,945
University of Chemistry and Technology – 4,189
Police Academy of the Czech Republic – 2,196
Academy of Arts, Architecture & Design (AAAD – UMPRUM) – 481
Academy of Performing Arts – 367
Academy of Fine Arts – 338
Total – 110,794

The numbers are taken from the annual reports of these universities for 2016. They also include 5,586 students of Charles University's three faculties based outside of Prague and 1,500 students of the one faculty of the University of Economics that is based outside of the city.

ABBREVIATIONS OF UNIVERSITIES IN PRAGUE

AMU = Academy of Performing Arts /Akademie múzických umění
    DAMU = Theatre Faculty / Divadelní fakulta
    FAMU = Film and TV Faculty at Academy of Performing Arts / Filmová
    a TV fakulta
    HAMU = Music Faculty at Academy of Performing Arts / Hudební fakulta
AVU = Academy of Fine Arts / Akademie výtvarných umění
CU = Charles University / Univerzita Karlova (UK)
    ETF = Protestant Theological Faculty / Evangelická teologická fakulta
    FF = Faculty of Arts / Filozofická fakulta
    FHS = Faculty of Humanities / Fakulta humanitních studií
    FSV = Faculty of Social Sciences / Fakulta sociálních věd
    FTVS = Faculty of Physical Education and Sport / Fakulta tělesné výchovy
    a sportu
    HTF = Hussite Theological Faculty / Husitská teologická fakulta
    KTF = Catholic Theological Faculty / Katolická teologická fakulta
    LF = Faculty of Medicine / Lékařská fakulta (1. LF, 2. LF, 3. LF)
    MFF = Faculty of Mathematics and Physics / Matematicko-fyzikální fakulta
    PedF = Faculty of Education / Pedagogická fakulta
    PF = Faculty of Law / Právnická fakulta
    PřF = Faculty of Science / Přírodovědecká fakulta
CULS = Czech University of Life Sciences / Česká zemědělská univerzita (ČZÚ)
CTU = Czech Technical University / České vysoké učení technické (ČVUT)
PA ČR = Police Academy of Czech Republic / Policejní akademie České republiky
UMPRUM = University of Decorative Arts (also known as Academy of Arts,
Architecture & Design – AAAD) / Vysoká škola uměleckoprůmyslová (VŠUP)
VŠCHT = University of Chemistry and Technology Prague / Vysoká škola
chemicko-technologická
VŠE = University of Economics Prague / Vysoká škola ekonomická

EMINENT PERSONS

Elizabeth of Pomerania (probably 1346–1393), fourth wife of Charles IV

Ferdinand I of Habsburg (1503–1564), Holy Roman emperor, king of Bohemia (1526–1564)

Ferdinand III of Habsburg (1608–1657), Holy Roman emperor, king of Bohemia and Hungary

Francis (Franz) I (1768–1835), king of Bohemia and Hungary, Holy Roman emperor (1792–1806, as Francis II), Austrian Emperor (1804–1835)

Joseph I of Habsburg (1678–1711), Holy Roman emperor, king of Bohemia (uncrowned) and Hungary

Joseph II of Habsburg-Lorraine (1741–1790), Holy Roman emperor, king of Bohemia (uncrowned) and Hungary

Charles I (1887–1922), last Austrian emperor, king of Bohemia and Hungary

Charles IV of Luxembourg (1316–1378), Bohemian and Roman king, from 1355 Holy Roman emperor

Charles VI of Habsburg (1685–1740), Holy Roman emperor

Leopold I of Habsburg (1640–1705), Holy Roman emperor, king of Bohemia and Hungary

Leopold II of Habsburg-Lorraine (1747–1792), Holy Roman emperor, king of Bohemia and Hungary

Louis XIV of Bourbon (1638–1715), French king

Maria Theresa (1717–1780), queen of Bohemia and Hungary, Austrian arch-duchess

Rudolf (Rudolph) II of Habsburg (1552–1612), king of Bohemia and Hungary, Holy Roman emperor

Wenceslas IV of Luxembourg (1361–1419), Bohemian and Roman king

St. Wenceslas (907–935), Czech saint, symbol of Czech statehood

Wilhelm II of Prussia (1859–1941), last German emperor

Albert, Eduard MUDr. (1841–1900), surgeon, professor in Vienna

Anděl, Bedřich (1821–1898), painter, lithographer and daguerreotypist.

Arnošt (Ernest) **of Pardubice** (1297?–1364), last Prague bishop and first Prague archbishop

Bacháček z Naiměřic, Martin (1539?–1612), mathematician and astronomer, rector of Prague university

Bareš, Pavel (1904–1984), architect

Bartoloměj z Chlumce known as Master Claretus (probably 1320–1370), one of the first holders of the title of professor

Campanus Vodňanský, Jan (1572–1622), author, 1621 rector of Prague University

Copernicus, Nicolaus (1473–1543), Polish astronomer, philosopher and medical doctor

Fanta, Josef (1856–1954), architect of the 'National Theatre generation', regarded as the creator of Czech art nouveau architecture

Frágner, Jaroslav (1898–1967), important architect, painter and town planner, pupil of Josef Gočár and university professor in the first half of the 20th century

Franta, Petr (born 1948), Czech architect, active in Canada and USA 1977–1991; after his return from abroad, founded his own studio in Prague

Frič, Josef Václav (1829–1890), author and journalist, radical activist in the student movement and student associations in the years 1848–49. Imprisoned, he spent part of his life in exile

Gerstner, František Josef (1756–1832), professor of mathematics, hydraulics and mechanics, first director of the Royal Bohemian Estates Technical Institute in Prague

Hájek of Hájek, Tadeáš (1525–1600), natural scientist, astronomer, mathematician, court doctor

Hanuš of Milheim (died 1405), courtier of Wenceslas IV, benefactor of Prague University

of Harrach, Ernst Adalbert (1598–1667), cardinal, from 1623 archbishop of Prague

Jadwiga of Anjou (1374–1399), Polish and Lithuanian queen, in 1397 financed foundation of Lithuanian College for Catholic clerics at Prague University, beatified in 1997

Heinsch, Johann Georg (1647–1712), Baroque painter who painted mostly religious subjects

Herget, František Antonín Leonard (1741–1800), professor of mathematics and engineering, deputy of the Bohemian Estates Land Diet

Heyrovský, Jaroslav (1890–1967), professor of physical chemistry, awarded Nobel Prize in 1959 for discoveries in polarography

Hlávka, Josef (1831–1908), architect, building entrepreneur, benefactor of the arts and education

Horáková, Milada (1901–1950), democratic politician, sentenced to death in communist show-trial

Horn, Uffo (1817–1860), poet and dramatist, liberal, leading representative of student movement in 1848

Hostinský, Otakar (1847–1910), aesthetician, theorist of theatre and music from the realist school

Hrdlička, Aleš (1869–1943), world-famous Czech doctor and anthropologist who spent most of his life in the USA

Hus, Jan (Huss, John) (1371–1415), preacher and reformer, 1409–10 rector of Prague University, sentenced to be burnt at the stake by the Council of Constance

Ginsberg, Irwin Allen (1926–1997), American poet

Jahn, Jan Jakub Quirin (1739–1802), painter, theoretician and historian of art, founder of the Society of Patriotic Friends of Art

Jeroným Pražský (Jerome of Prague) (1379–1416), Czech theologian and philosopher, adherent of John Wycliffe, burnt at the stake in Constance after Jan Hus

Jesenský (Jessenius), Jan (1566–1621), Slovak doctor, 1617–20 rector of Prague University and politician in the service of the Czech estates, executed in 1621 along with other leaders of the revolt

Kauffer of Sturmwehr, Jan Jiří (?), lawyer, commander of student cohort in the defence of Prague against the Swedes in 1648

Kelly, Edward (1555–1597), English alchemist at the court of Rudolf II

Kepler, Johannes (1571–1630), German mathematician, astronomer and optician at the court of Rudolf II

Klokner, František (1872–1960), professor of statics, civil engineering and iron-concrete buildings

Kolář, František (1825–1894), painter, illustrator, graphic artist

Kolin (Collinus) **z Chotěřiny,** Matouš (1516–1566), humanist poet and man of learning

Kořistka, Karel František Edvard (1825–1906), cartographer, topographer and statistician, professor of mathematics at Prague Polytechnic, politician

Kotěra, Jan (1871–1923), architect

Krafft-Steiner, Barbara (1764–1825), painter

Krásnohorská, Eliška (Alžběta Pechová, 1847–1926), author, propagator of women's education and schooling for girls

Krocín z Drahobejle, Václav (1532–1905), mayor of Prague's Old Town in the years 1584–1605, benefactor

Kříž, Václav (around 1400), wealthy merchant, Old Town burgher, benefactor

Kuntz, Antonín (died 1769), Baroque architect and builder

Langweil, Antonín (1791–1837), university librarian at Klementinum, maker of paper model of historic Prague

Lanna, Vojtěch (1836–1909), industrialist and benefactor

Lauda, Jan (1898–1959), sculptor

Louda (Lauda) z Chlumčan, Matěj (d. 1460), Hussite warrior and diplomat

Lumbe, Josef (1801–1879), professor at the polytechnic, expert on agricultural education

Lurago, Carlo (1618–1684), architect and builder

Lurago, Francesco Anselmo (1634–1693), builder

Mádl, Karel Boromejský (1859–1932), historian and art critic

Mácha, Karel Hynek (1810–1836), poet, representative of Czech Romanticism

Machek, Antonín (1775–1844), painter, mainly of portraits

Machoň, Ladislav (1888–1973), architect

Machytka, Jan (1844–1887), architect

Mánes, Josef (1820–1871), painter, founder of modern Czech painting

Marci, Jan Marcus (1595–1667), natural scientist and philosopher

Martinů, Bohuslav (1890–1959), famous Czech composer of the modernist era

Mařák, Julius (1832–1899), landscape painter, draughtsman and graphic artist

Masaryk, Tomáš Garrigue (1850–1937), professor of sociology and philosophy, politician, first Czechoslovak president

Mašek, Karel Vítězslav (1865–1927), architect and painter

Max, Josef (1804–1855), sculptor

Melanchton, Philipp (1497–1560), German humanist man of learning, reformist theologian

Mikan, Josef Bohumír (1743–1814), doctor, botanist, founder of Prague University's botanical garden

Mladota ze Solopysk, Ferdinand Antonín (1652–1726), knight

Myslbek, Josef Václav (1848–1922), sculptor

of Nepomuk, John, St. (1345–1393), vicar-general of Prague archbishop, beatified in 1729

von Neurath, Konstantin (1873–1956), German Nazi politician, in the years 1939–1943 imperial protector of the Protectorate of Bohemia and Moravia

Neuräutter, Augustin (?), engraver from beginning of 18th century

Newton, Isaac (1643–1727), famous English philosopher, physicist, mathematician and astronomer

Ondřej, Severin (1889–1964), architect

Opletal, Jan (1915–1939), student of Faculty of Medicine at CU, fatally wounded in demonstration on 28 October 1939

Orsi, Giovanni Domenico (1633?–1679), architect and builder

Palach, Jan (1948–1969), student of Philosophy Faculty at CU, who voluntarily set himself on fire in order to wake up society from its resignation toward the occupation by Warsaw Pact forces

Palaeologus, Jacobus (1520–1585), Greek monk living in exile, later burned by the inquisition as a heretic

Patočka, Jan (1907–1977), important philosopher, one of the spokespersons of Charter 77

Perjovschi, Dan (b. 1961), Rumanian artist and journalist, author of sketched decoration at the National Library of Technology in Prague

Peters, Otto (1882–1970), portrait painter and figurative artist

Petřík, Theodor (1882–1961), architect

Plachý, Jiří (1606–1664), Jesuit, defender of Prague against the Swedes in 1648

Plečnik, Josip (1872–1957), Slovenian architect

Plichta, Jan (1891–1975), important sport personality in the First Republic period

le Prestre de Vauban, Sébastien (1633–1707), French builder of military fortifications

Purkyně, Jan Evangelista (1787–1869), physiologist, anatomist, biologist and philosopher

Reček, Jan (?), mayor of Prague's Old Town, founder of university college in 1438

Reiner, Martin (c.1627–1680), early-Baroque builder, grandfather of painter V. V. Reinera

Rieger, František Ladislav (1818–1903), politician of Old Czech party, editor-in-chief of first Czech general encyclopedia in 11 volumes

Roštlapil, Václav (1856–1930), architect

Rotlev, Johlin (?), Prague burgher, master of the royal mint and banker, owner of house known as U Červeného lva (Red Lion) in the middle of the 14th century

Ruben, Kristián (1805–1875), painter

Růžičková, Věra (born 1924), sculptor

Sakař, Josef (1856–1936), architect

Semper, Gottfried (1803–1879), German architect

Schmoranz, František jr. (1845–1892), architect

Schmoranz, Josef (1855–1938), painter and designer, administrator of artistic collections and art theorist

Schor, Jan Ferdinand (1686–1767), painter and landscape architect, professor at the Estates Engineering School

Skuherský, Rudolf (1828–1863), mathematician, professor of descriptive geometry at the polytechnic, where he advocated granting the Czech language equal status to that of German in teaching

Smetana, Augustin (1814–1851), philosopher of the Hegel school, active participant in the revolutionary movement in 1848.

Smotlacha, František (1884–1956), mycologist and founder of Czech university sport

Sychra, Vladimír (1903–1963), painter

Šaloun, Ladislav (1870–1946), sculptor

Šantavý, Tomáš (born 1951), architect

Šrámková, Alena (born 1929), architect

Šternberk-Manderscheid, František Josef (1763–1830), benefactor of art, enlightenment thinker, one of the founders of the Patriotic Museum

Štursa, Jan (1880–1925), sculptor, significant representative of Czech art nouveau

Teinitzerová, Marie (1879–1960), textile artist

Thun-Hohenstein, Leopold (1811–1888), Czech and Austrian politician, as minister of culture and education carried out a number of number of educational reforms according to the German model

Tomek, Vác(s)lav Vladivoj (1818–1905), historian

Tyrš, Miroslav (1832–1884), art historian, aesthetician, initiator of organized physical education, founder of Sokol (Czech gymnastics association)

Ullmann, Vojtěch Ignác (1822–1897), architect

Vacková, Růžena (1901–1982), classical archaeologist, excluded from university career after 1948 on account of her democratic stances

Vencovský, František (1923–2006), economist

Volckmann, Martin Xavier (?), author, in 1672 celebrated the victory of the Counter-Reformation at Charles-Ferdinand University

Wiehl, Antonín (1846–1910), architect

Willenberg, Christian Josef (1655?–1731), civil engineer, first professor at the Estates Engineering School in Prague, which is the precursor of the CTU

Windisch-Graetz (Windischgrätz), Alfred (1787–1862), field marshall and Bohemian estates nobleman, as commanding general in Bohemia he suppressed the revolutionary movement in 1848

Zalužanský, Adam (1555–1613), humanist, doctor, pharmacist, botanist

Zasche, Josef (1875–1957), architect

Zeidler, Jeroným Josef (1790–1870), politician, abbot of Strahov Monastery, repeatedly elected rector of Charles-Ferdinand University

Zelenka, Jan Dismas (1679–1745), composer of High Baroque period

Zoubek, Olbram (1926–2017), sculptor

ACKNOWLEDGEMENTS

Karolinum Press would like to thank the administrators of artistic and historical collections for their kindness in providing pictures for this publication and for their consent to the reproduction of these pictures.

MAP REFERENCES

1. Karolinum – rectorate of Charles University (CU), Ovocný trh 5 (Fruit Market), Prague 1
2. Angels' College – Romanesque cellar, U Radnice 3, Prague 1
3. Klementinum, Křižovnická 2, Prague 1
4. Faculty of Arts, CU – dean's office, nám. Jana Palacha 2 (Jan Palach Square), Prague 1
5. Faculty of Law, CU – dean's office, nám. Curieových 7 (Curies Square), Prague 1
6. Faculty of Education, CU – dean's office, M. D. Rettigové 4, Prague 2
7. Faculty of Natural Sciences, CU – dean's office, Albertov 6, Prague 2
8. Botanical garden of Charles University, Na Slupi 16, Prague 2
9. Faculty of Mathematics and Physics, CU – dean's office, Ke Karlovu 3, Prague 2
10. Jesuit professed house and St. Wenceslas rotunda, Malostranské nám 25 (Lesser Town Square), Prague 1
11. Building of the Faculty of Mathematics and Physics, CU, V Holešovičkách 2, Prague 8
12. First Faculty of Medicine, CU – dean's office, Prague 2, Kateřinská 32
13. Former Jesuit College of St. Ignatius, Karlovo nám (Charles Square), Prague 2
14. Faust House, Karlovo nám. 502–503/40, , Prague 2
15. Royal Bohemian Maternity Hospital, U Apolináře, Apolinářská 18, Prague 2
16. Second Faculty of Medicine, CU – dean's office, V Úvalu 84, Prague 5
17. Third Faculty of Medicine, CU – dean's office, Ruská 87, Prague 10
18. Catholic Theological Faculty, CU – dean's office, Thákurova 3, Prague 6
19. Protestant Theological Faculty, CU – dean's office, Černá ul. 9/646, Prague 1
20. Hussite Theological Faculty, CU – dean's office, Pacovská 350, Prague 4
21. Faculty of Social Sciences, CU – dean's office, Smetanovo nábř. 6/995, Prague 1
22. Faculty of Humanities, CU – dean's office, U Kříže 8, Prague 5
23. Faculty of Physical Education and Sport, CU – dean's office, José Martího 31, Prague 6
24. Strahov Halls of Residence, Vaníčkova 315/7, Prague 6
25. Lusatian Seminary, U Lužického semináře 90/1, Prague 1
26. Royal Bohemian Estates Engineering School – Czech Technical University (CTU), Husova 5, Prague 1
27. Czech Polytechnic – CTU, Karlovo nám. 13, Prague 2
28. Faculty of Transportation Sciences, CTU, Konviktská 20, Prague 1
29. Czech Technical University building, Zikova 4, Prague 6
30. Bethlehem Chapel, Betlémské náměstí 5, Prague 1
31. Faculty of Nuclear Sciences and Physical Engineering, CTU, Břehová 7, Prague 1
32. CTU campus, Thákurova 7–9, Prague 6
33. Academy of Fine Arts (AVU), U Akademie 4, Prague 7
34. Šaloun art studio, AVU, Slovenská 4, Prague 10
35. Modern Gallery, AVU, U starého výstaviště 188, Prague 7
36. University of Decorative Arts (UMPRUM – AAAD) – rectorate, nám. Jana Palacha 3, Prague 1
37. Lichtenstein Palace – rectorate of Academy of Performing Arts (AMU) and Music and Dance Faculty (HAMU), Malostranské nám. 12–13, Prague 1
38. Kokořovský Palace – dean's office of Faculty of Theatre at AMU, Karlova 26 / Řetězová 5, Prague 1
39. Lažanský Palace – dean's office FAMU, Smetanovo nábř. 2, Prague 1
40. Grébovka Villa – Czech University of Life Sciences (CULS), Havlíčkovy sady 58, Prague 2
41. CULS – rectorate and pleasure garden, Kamýcká 129, Prague 6
42. CULS, Kamýcká 1176, Prague 6
43. University of Chemistry and Technology – rectorate, Technická 5, Prague 6
44. University of Economics – rectorate, nám. W. Churchilla 4, U Rajské zahrady 3, Prague 3
45. Police Academy of Czech Republic – rectorate, Lhotecká 559/7, Prague 4
46. National Library of Technology, Technická 2710/6, Prague 6

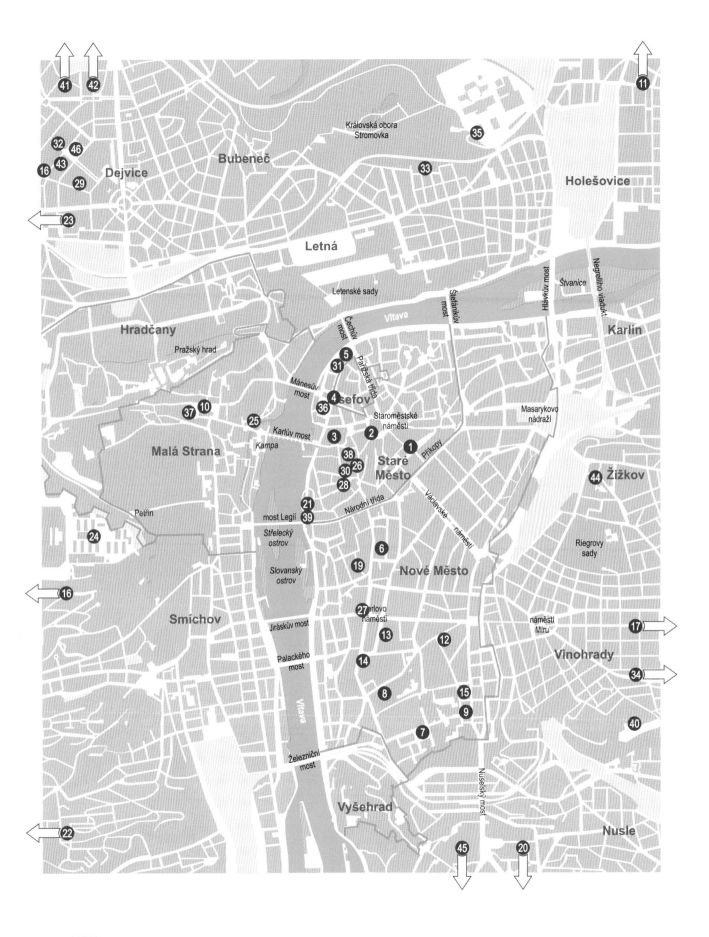

LIST OF ILLUSTRATIONS

Cover: St. John the Evangelist – Theological Hall of the Strahov Library, photo Oto Palán; Karolinum – Baroque portal, photo Oto Palán
Inside cover: Klementinum tower, photo Oto Palán
Opening pages: pp. 2–3: Ceiling of vestibule of Faculty of Law CU, photo Martin Micka; p. 7: Betlehem Chapel, photo Oto Palán; p. 8: Gothic oriel at Karolinum, photo Oto Palán; p. 10–11: Karolinum's main entrance, photo Oto Palán; p. 12: Master Jan Hus at the pulpit – Antithesis Christi et Antichristi (Jena codex). Collection of the National Museum – National Museum Library, IV B 24, fol. 37v.

Documentary Sources of Illustrations
Unless stated otherwise, illustrations used are from Charles University sources

Prague University Town – Illustrated Guide

Frontispiece: View from astronomical tower at Klementinum

1U/ Otto Peters: T. G. Masaryk, 1932, photo Oto Palán

1V/ Aula Minor, photo Oto Palán

1X/ Inner courtyard, photo Oto Palán

1Y/ Karel Lidický: Statue of Jan Hus, 1957, photo Oto Palán

1Z/ Façade of Karolinum from Železná Street, photo Oto Palán

2/ FACULTY OF ARTS CU

2A/ Façade of dean's office building, photo Oto Palán

2B/ Stairs in main building of the faculty with statue of T. G. Masaryk on landing, photo Oto Palán

2C/ Memorial plaque to Jan Palach on façade of Faculty of Arts, photo Oto Palán

3/ FACULTY OF LAW CU

3A/ Façade of dean's office building, photo Oto Palán

3B/ Hall of Faculty of Law building, photo Martin Micka

3C/ Collegium Maximum (Aula Maxima), photo Martin Micka

4/ FACULTY OF EDUCATION CU – dean's office building, photo Oto Palán

5/ FACULTY OF SCIENCE CU

5A/ Façade of dean's office building, photo Oto Palán

5B/ Stairs, photo Oto Palán

5D/ Albert Einstein – memorial plaque, photo Oto Palán

5C/ Jaroslav Heyrovský – memorial plaque, photo Oto Palán

5E–F/ Botanical garden, photo Oto Palán

6/ FACULTY OF MATHEMATICS AND PHYSICS CU

6A/ Façade of dean's office building, photo Martin Micka

6B/ Jesuit professed house – façade, photo Martin Micka

6C/ Jesuit professed house – graduation hall, photo Oto Palán

6D/ Rotunda computer laboratory, photo Oto Palán

6E/ St. Wenceslas Rotunda, photo Martin Micka

6F/ Astronomy Institute CU, photo Martin Micka

7/ FIRST FACULTY OF MEDICINE CU

7A/ Façade of dean's office, photo Oto Palán

7B/ Former Jesuit College, photo Martin Micka

7C/ Faust House, photo Martin Micka

7D/ Royal Bohemian Maternity Hospital U Apolináře, photo Martin Micka

8/ SECOND FACULTY OF MEDICINE CU – dean's office, photo Oto Palán

9/ THIRD FACULTY OF MEDICINE CU – dean's office, photo Oto Palán

10/ CATHOLIC THEOLOGICAL FACULTY CU

10A/ Dean's office building, photo Oto Palán

10B–C/ Chapel interior, photo Martin Micka

10D/ CTF aula, photo Martin Micka

11/ PROTESTANT THEOLOGICAL FACULTY Theological Faculty– dean's office, photo Oto Palán

12/ HUSSITE THEOLOGICAL FACULTY CU – dean's office, photo Oto Palán

13/ FACULTY OF SOCIAL SCIENCES CU – dean's office (known as Hollar building), photo Oto Palán

14/ FACULTY OF HUMANITIES CU – dean's office, photo Oto Palán

15/ FACULTY OF PHYSICAL EDUCATION AND SPORT CU – dean's office, photo Oto Palán

16/ KLEMENTINUM

16A/ Baroque entrance from Mariánské nám., photo Oto Palán

16B/ Baroque hall, photo Czech National Library, Eva Hodíková

16C/ Summer refectory, photo Czech National Library, Eva Hodíková

16D/ Révové nádvoří (Vine Court), photo Oto Palán

16E/ Statue of student in courtyard, photo Oto Palán
16F/ Astronomical tower, photo Oto Palán
16G/ Entrance from Charles Bridge and façade of Church of the Holy Saviour (St. Salvator), photo Oto Palán
17/ LUSATIAN SEMINARY, photo Martin Micka
18/ STRAHOV HALLS OF RESIDENCE, photo Martin Micka

19/ CZECH TECHNICAL UNIVERSITY
19A/ CTU – rectorate and Czech Institute of Informatics, Robotics and Cybernetics (CIIRK), photo Martin Micka
19B/ Royal Bohemian Estates Technical Institute (Husova Street), photo Martin Micka
19C–D/ Czech Polytechnic (Karlovo nám.), photo Martin Micka
19E/ Faculty of Transportation Sciences (Konviktská Street), photo Martin Micka
19F/ Faculty of Nuclear Sciences and Physical Engineering (Břehová Street), photo Martin Micka
19G/ Faculty of Architecture (Thákurova Street), photo Martin Micka
19H/ Klokner Institute (Zikova Street), photo Martin Micka
19I/ Bethlehem Chapel – exterior, photo Oto Palán
19J /Bethlehem Chapel – interior, photo Martin Micka

20/ ACADEMY OF FINE ARTS
20A/ AVU building – rectorate, photo Martin Micka
20B/ School of Architecture, photo Martin Micka
20C–D/ Modern Gallery at AVU, photo Martin Micka
20E/ Šaloun atelier at AVU, photo Věroslav Škrabánek

21/ UNIVERSITY OF DECORATIVE ARTS
21A/ UMPRUM (AAAD) building – rectorate, photo Martin Micka
21B/ Bust of Jan Kotěra on building's façade, photo Martin Micka
21C–D/ UMPRUM studios, photo Martin Micka

22/ ACADEMY OF PERFORMING ARTS
22A–B/ rectorate and HAMU – Lichtenstein Palace, photo Martin Micka
22C/ Faculty of Theatre – Kokořovský Palace, photo Martin Micka
22D/ DISK Theatre, photo Martin Micka
22E/ Faculty of Film and TV– Lažanský Palace, photo Martin Micka

23/ CZECH UNIVERSITY OF LIFE SCIENCES
23A/ CULS building – rectorate, photo Martin Micka
23B/ Pleasure garden in complex, photo Martin Micka
23C/ Faculty of Forestry and Wood Sciences, photo Martin Micka
23D/ Grébovka Villa, photo Martin Micka

24/ UNIVERSITY OF CHEMISTRY AND TECHNOLOGY – rectorate building, photo Martin Micka

25/ UNIVERSITY OF ECONOMICS
25A/ University of Economics – entrance façade, photo Martin Micka
25B/ Interior, photo Martin Micka
25C/ Vencovský Aula in so-called New Building, photo Martin Micka

26/ POLICE ACADEMY CR, photo Martin Micka

27A–B/ NATIONAL LIBRARY OF TECHNOLOGY, photo Martin Micka

Prof. PhDr. JOSEF PETRÁŇ, CSc., Dr.h.c. (1930–2017)

Historian, professor of Charles University, author and co-author of numerous monographs and studies. At the beginning of his career he focused on economic and social history and on developing an iconographic method. He made a substantial contribution to the study of material culture of the early-modern period and to modern methods of regional studies. Later he concentrated on the history of Charles University and in particular its Faculty of Arts.

Among his published works:

Karolinum a historické koleje Univerzity Karlovy v Praze (with A. Kubíček and A. Petráňová). Prague, SNKLU 1961

Zemědělská výroba v Čechách ve druhé polovině 16. a počátkem 17. století. Prague, SPN 1963

Poddaný lid v Čechách na prahu třicetileté války. Prague, Nakladatelství ČSAV 1963

Homo faber (with V. Husa and A. Šubrtová). Prague, Academia 1967

Český znak. Prague, Ministerstvo kultury 1970

Staroměstská exekuce. Prague, MF 1972 (2. ed. Brána 1985, 3. ed. MF 1995, 4. ed. Rodiče 2004)

Rebelie. Příběh jednoho týdne a dvou dní v březnu roku 1775. Prague, ČS 1975

Nástin dějin filosofické fakulty Univerzity Karlovy do roku 1948. Prague, Charles University 1984

Pozdně Gothic umění v Čechách (co-author). Prague, Odeon 1984 (2. ed. 1985)

Kalendář. Velký stavovský ples v Nosticově Národním divadle v Praze dne 12. září 1791. Prague, ČS 1988 (2. ed. NLN 2004)

Dějiny hmotné kultury I/1-2, II/1-2 (main author and editor). Prague, SPN a Karolinum 1985–1998

Univerzitní slavnosti v Karolinu. Prague, Univerzita Karlova 1991

Dějiny Univerzity Karlovy I–IV (editor-in-chief and author of some chapters). Prague, Charles University 1995–1998

Památky Univerzity Karlovy (editor and author of some chapters). Prague, Karolinum 1999

Příběh Ouběnic v podblanické krajině. Mikrohistorie české vesnice. Ouběnice, NLN 2000 (2. ed. Prague 2001)

Dvacáté století v Ouběnicích. Prague, NLN 2009

Karolinum. Prague, Karolinum 2010 (Eng. 2010)

České dějiny ve znamení kultury (selected studies). Pardubice, Univerzita Pardubice 2010 (ed. J. Pánek and P. Vorel)

Dějiny českého venkova v příběhu Ouběnic. Prague, NLN 2011

Filozofové dělají revoluci. Filozofická fakulta Univerzity Karlovy během komunistického experimentu (1948–1968–1989). Prague, Karolinum 2015

Rolník v tradiční evropské kultuře. Prague, Set Out 2000 (with Lydia Petráňová)

Čestní doktoři Univerzity Karlovy. Prague, Karolinum 2017 (with Lydia Petráňová)

Doc. PhDr. LYDIA PETRÁŇOVÁ, CSc. (born 1941)

Lydia Petráňová works at the Ethnological Institute of the Czech Academy of Sciences in the department of historical ethnology. She is an expert in the field of traditional material and spiritual folk culture, including the symbolism of Prague's historic streets. She collaborated with Josef Petráň for many years.

Among her published works:
Domovní znamení staré Prahy. Prague, Panorama 1988 (2. ed. Panorama 1991, 3. ed. Academia 2008)
50 Bilder aus Böhmen und Mähren. Prag, Panorama 1992
Bilder aus Prag. Prag, Academia – Panorama 1995
Průvodce všedním životem ve středověku. Praguc – Úvaly, Albra 2005
Lidová kultura. Národopisná encyklopedie Čech, Moravy a Slezska (co-editor and author of some entries). Prague, MF 2007
Friedrich Julius Rottmann: Popis svatebních obyčejů u známých národů. Kritické vydání starého tisku. Prague, Ethnological Institute of the Czech Academy of Sciences, 2009
Velké dějiny zemí Koruny české. Tematická řada. Lidová kultura (spoluautorka). Prague – Litomyšl, Paseka 2014

This series is devoted to the history of Prague, with a focus on the arts and intellectual life of the city. In a factual yet lively way it seeks to give an informed account of the thousand-year development of the city with its changes, both intellectual and material, and its legendary *genius loci*, thus contributing to general knowledge about Czech culture. A typical volume in the series comprises a comprehensive account of the topic, accompanied by illustrations and 'walks through Prague', by means of photographs of the preserved historic architecture and other works of art together with commentary. The publication includes a list of important historical figures, an index with corresponding maps of the location of the art and architecture, and a bibliography. The contributors to this series are respected Prague art historians, photographers, and translators.